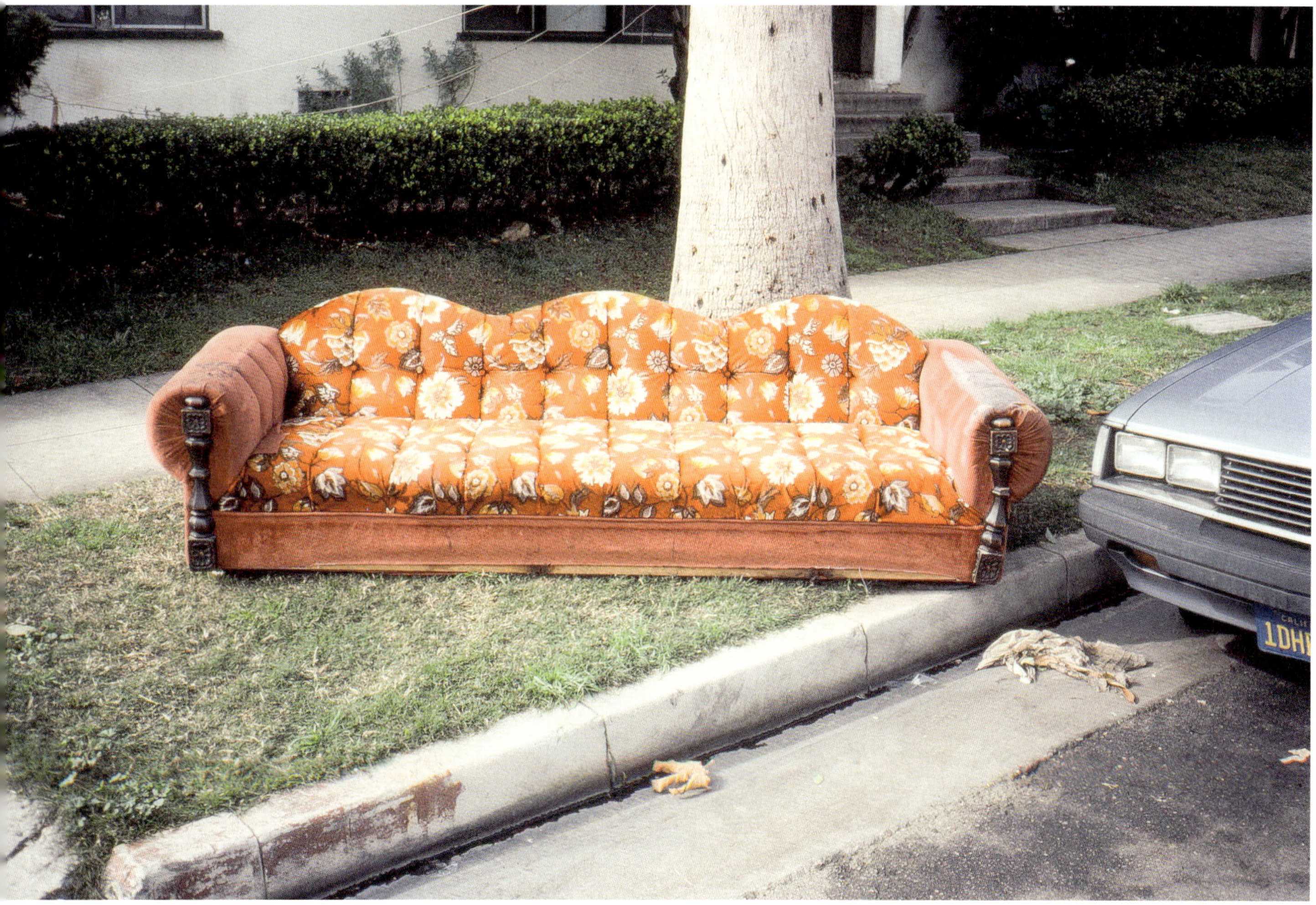

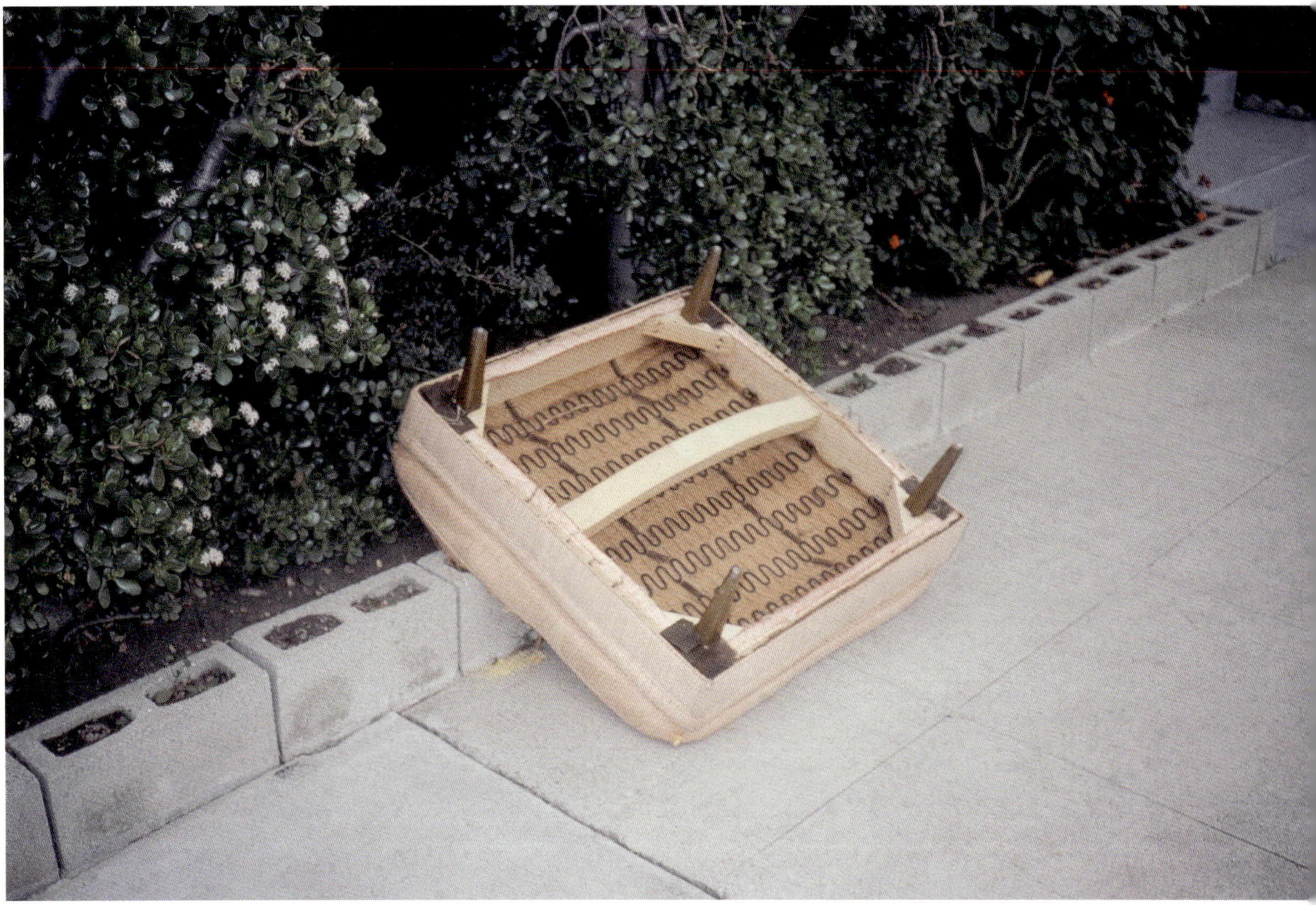

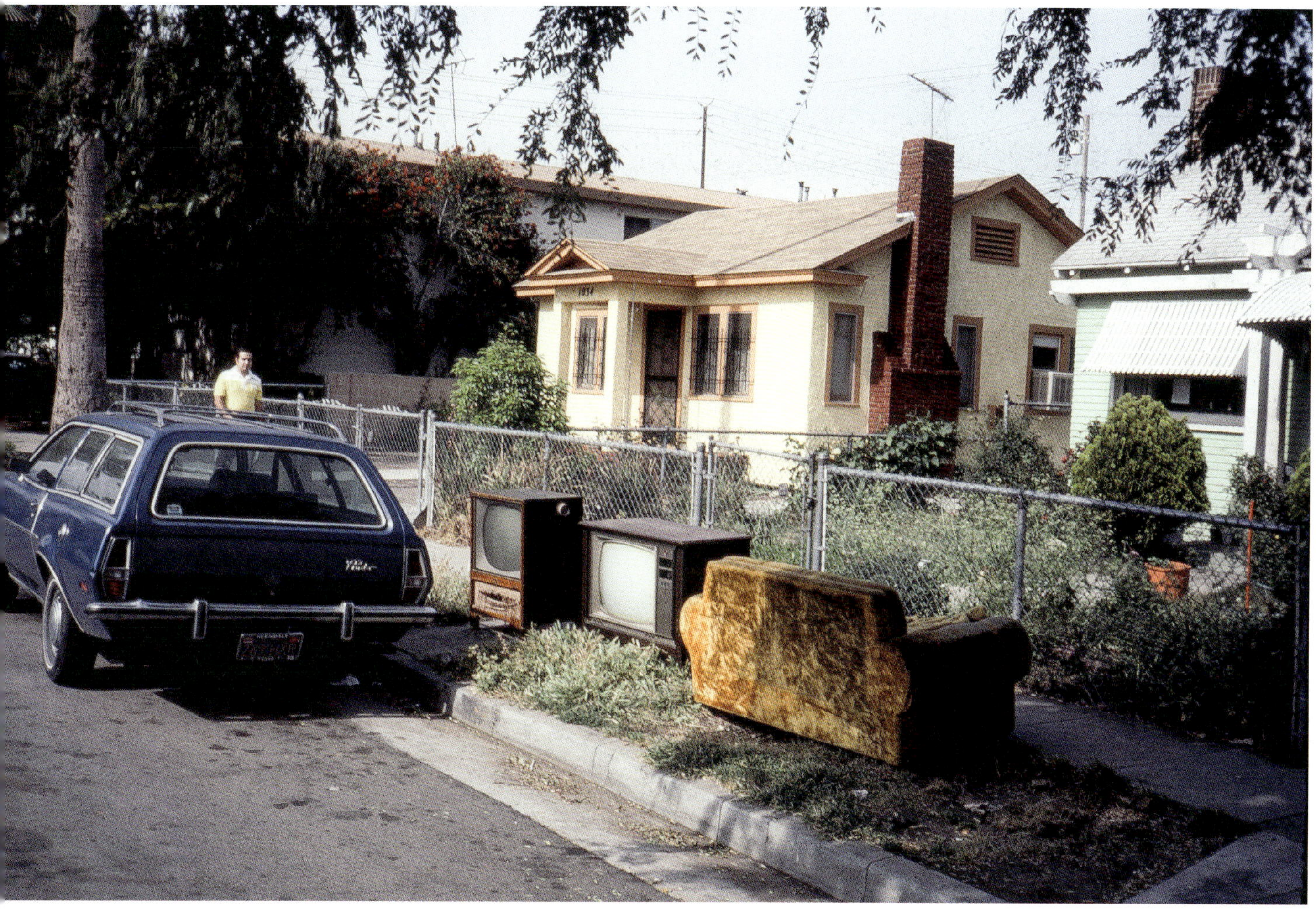
1034

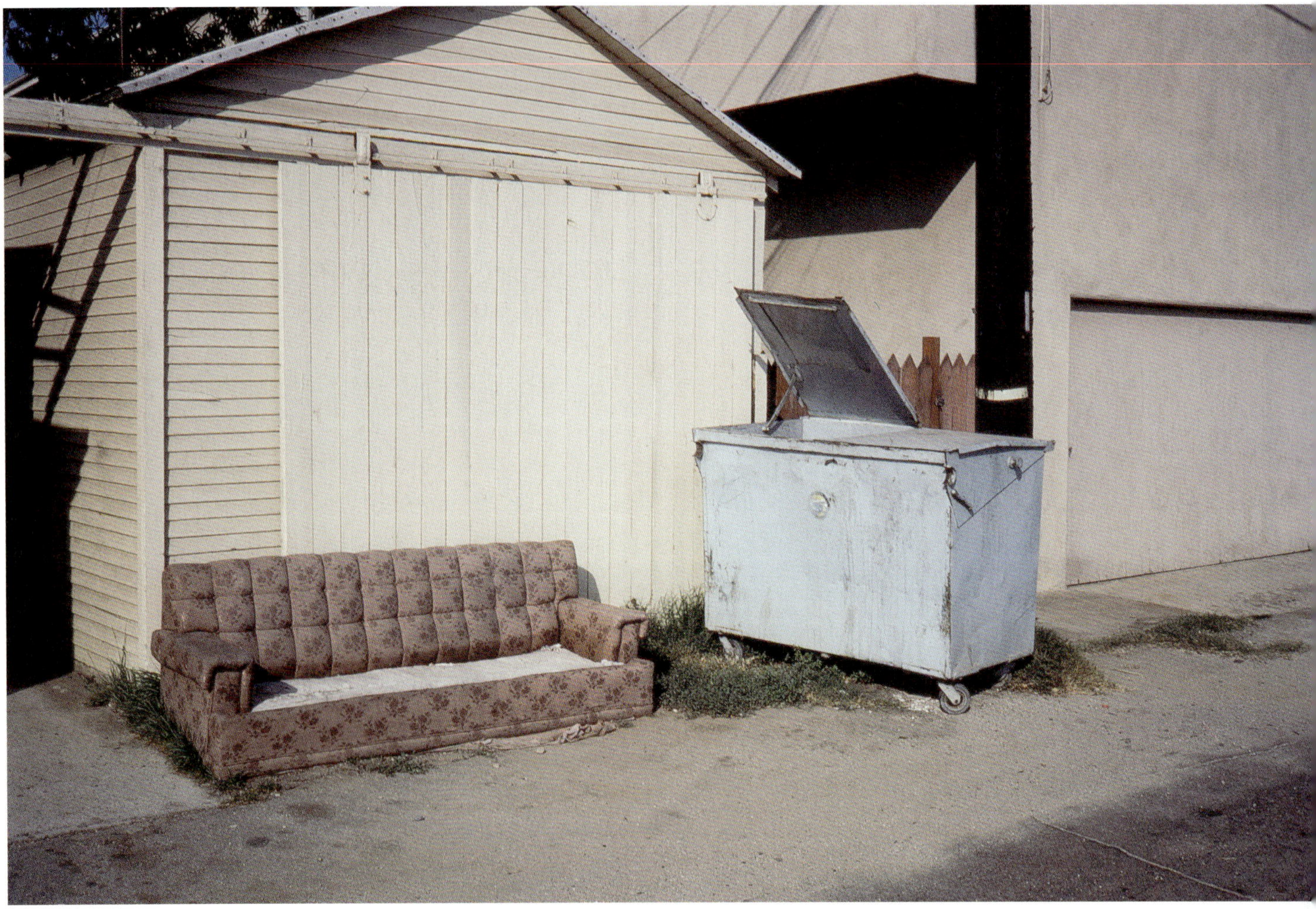

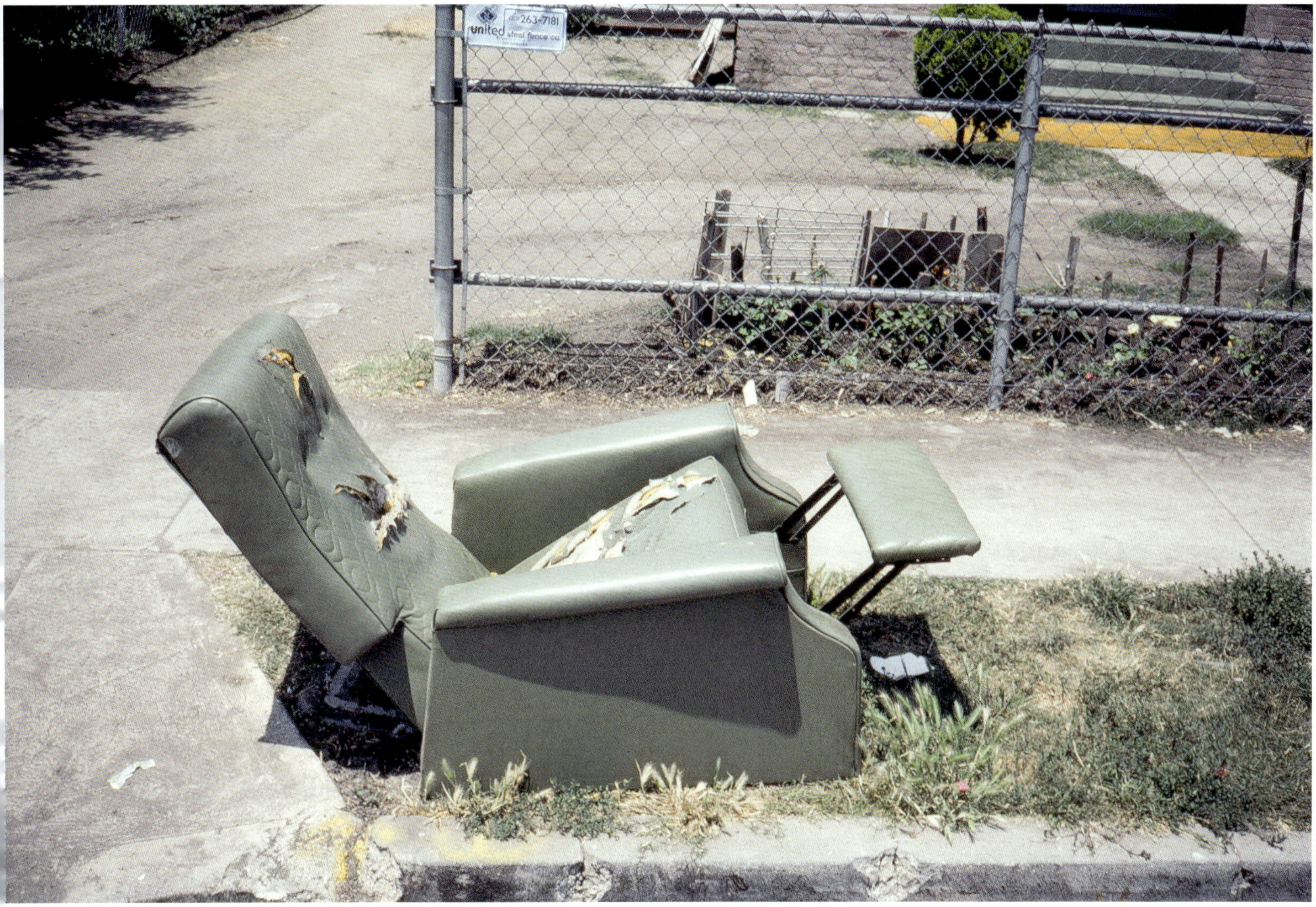
263-7181
united

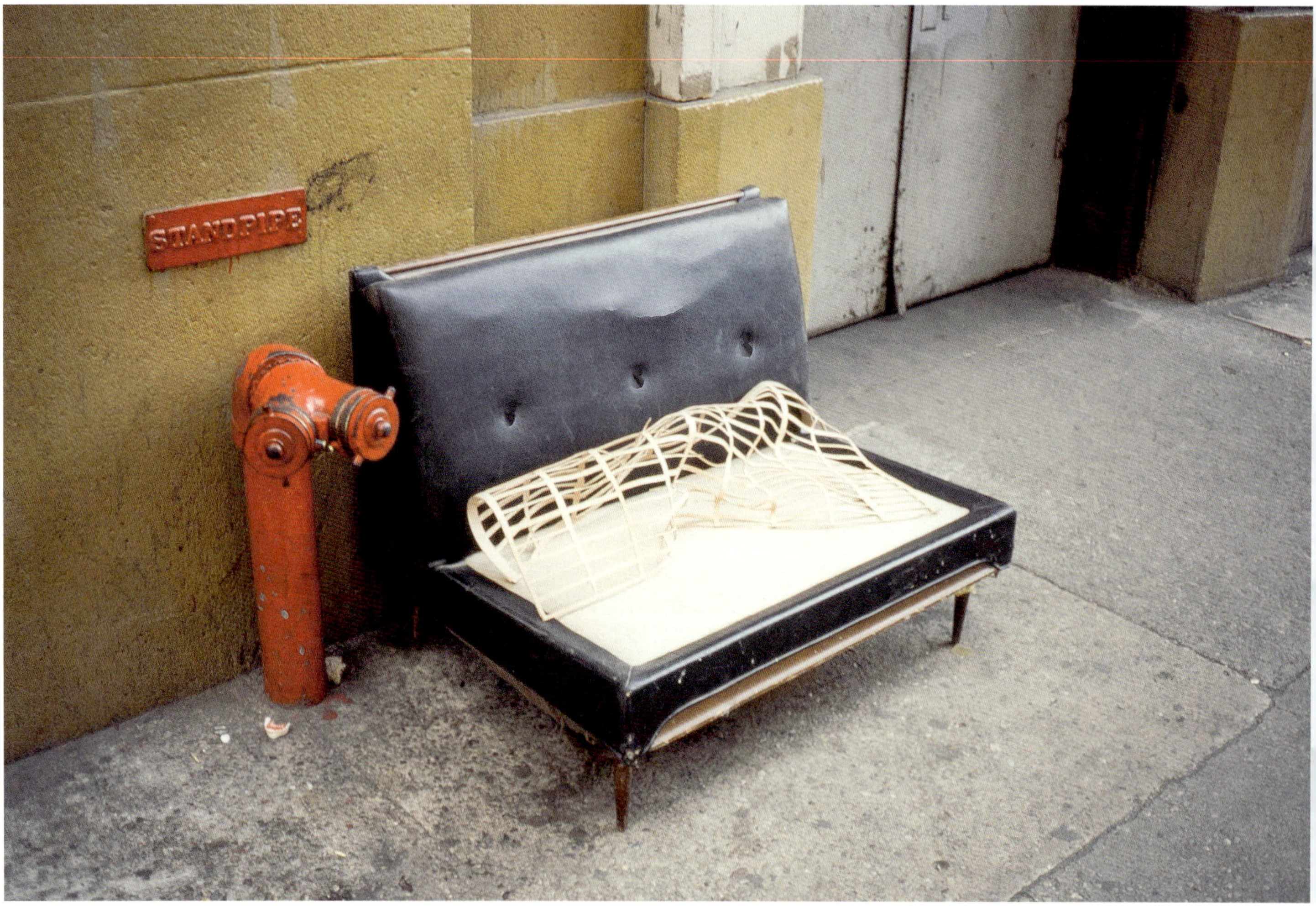
STANDPIPE

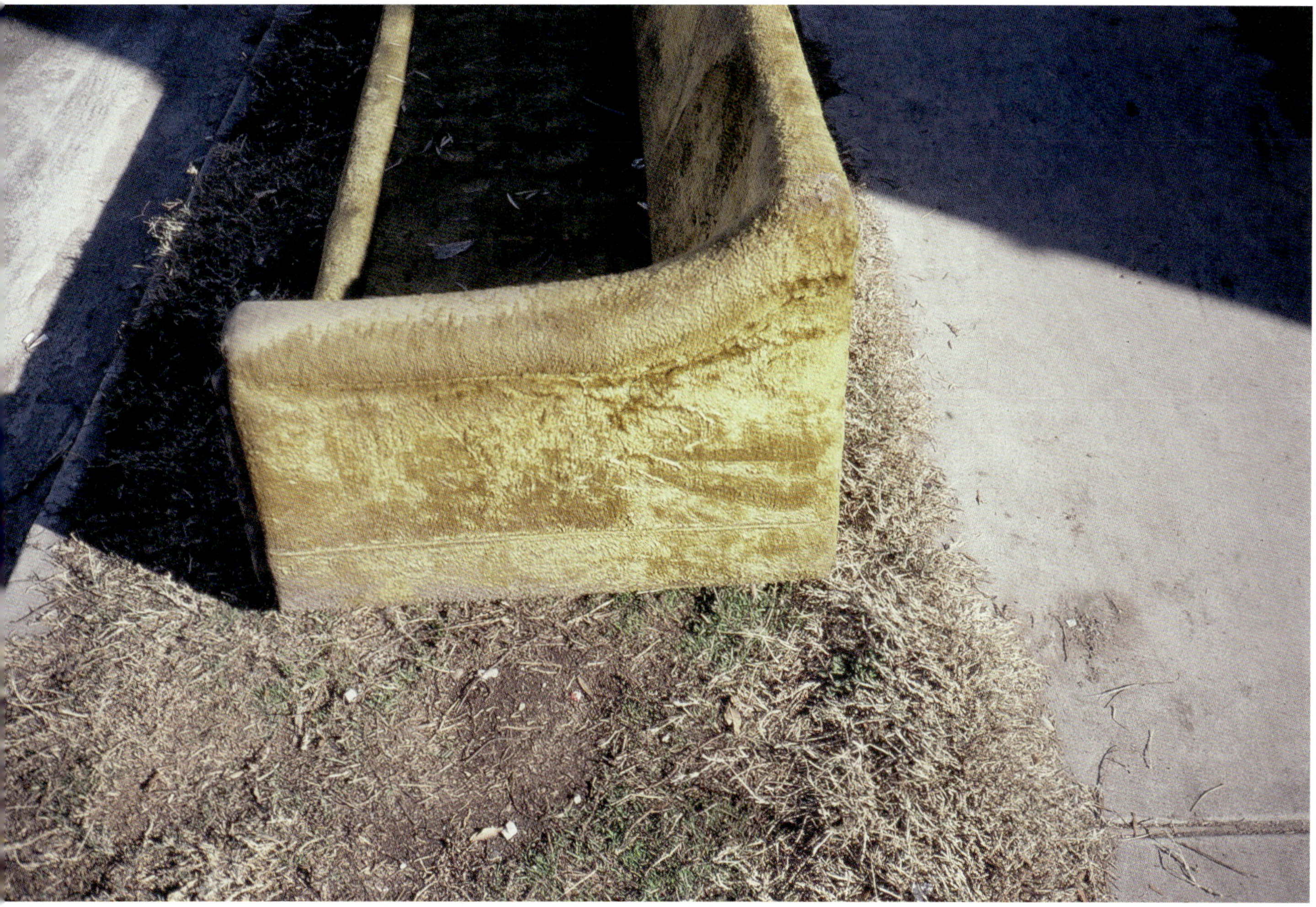

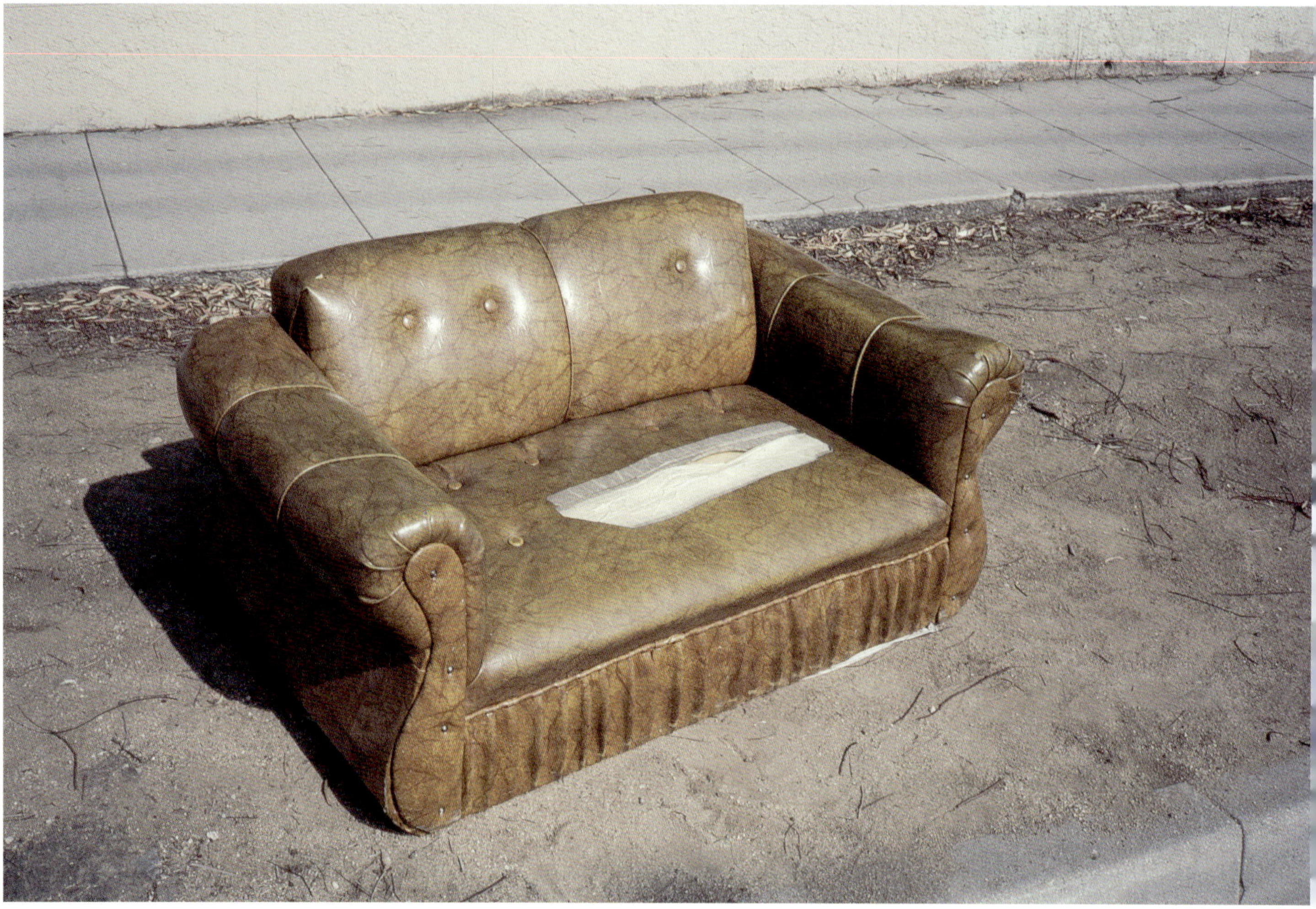

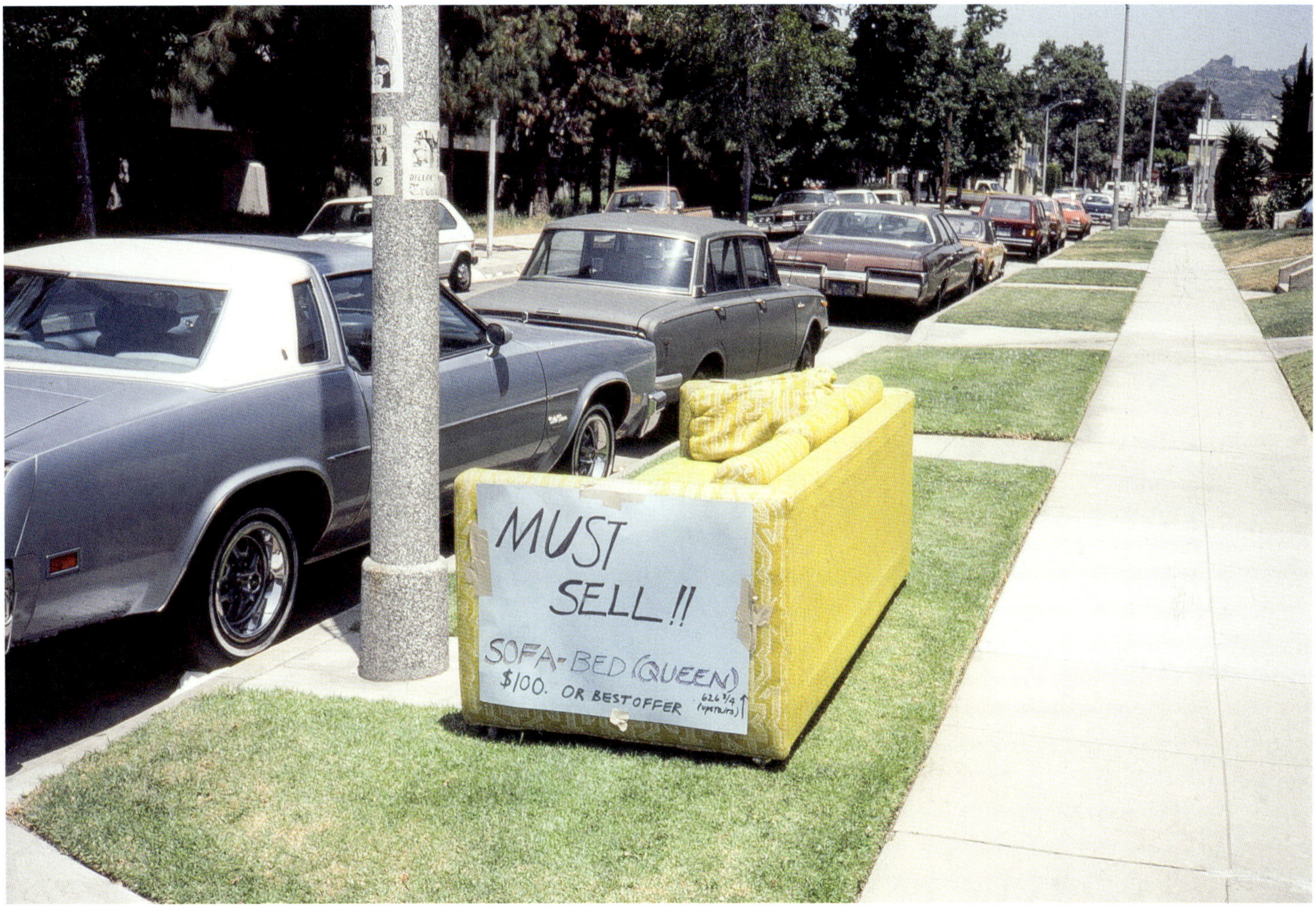
MUST
SELL!!
SOFA-BED (QUEEN)
$100. OR BEST OFFER

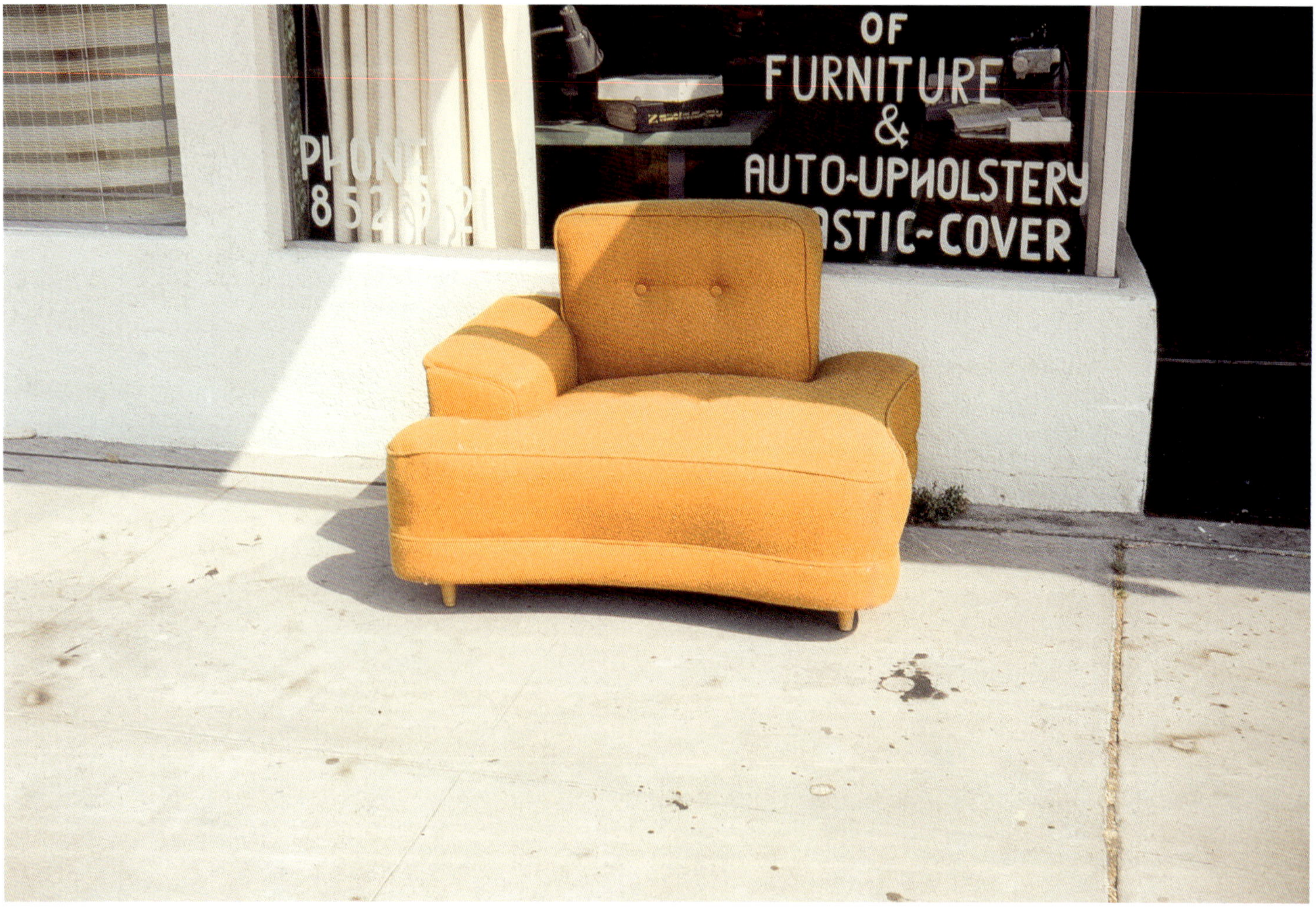
OF
FURNITURE
&
AUTO-UPHOLSTERY

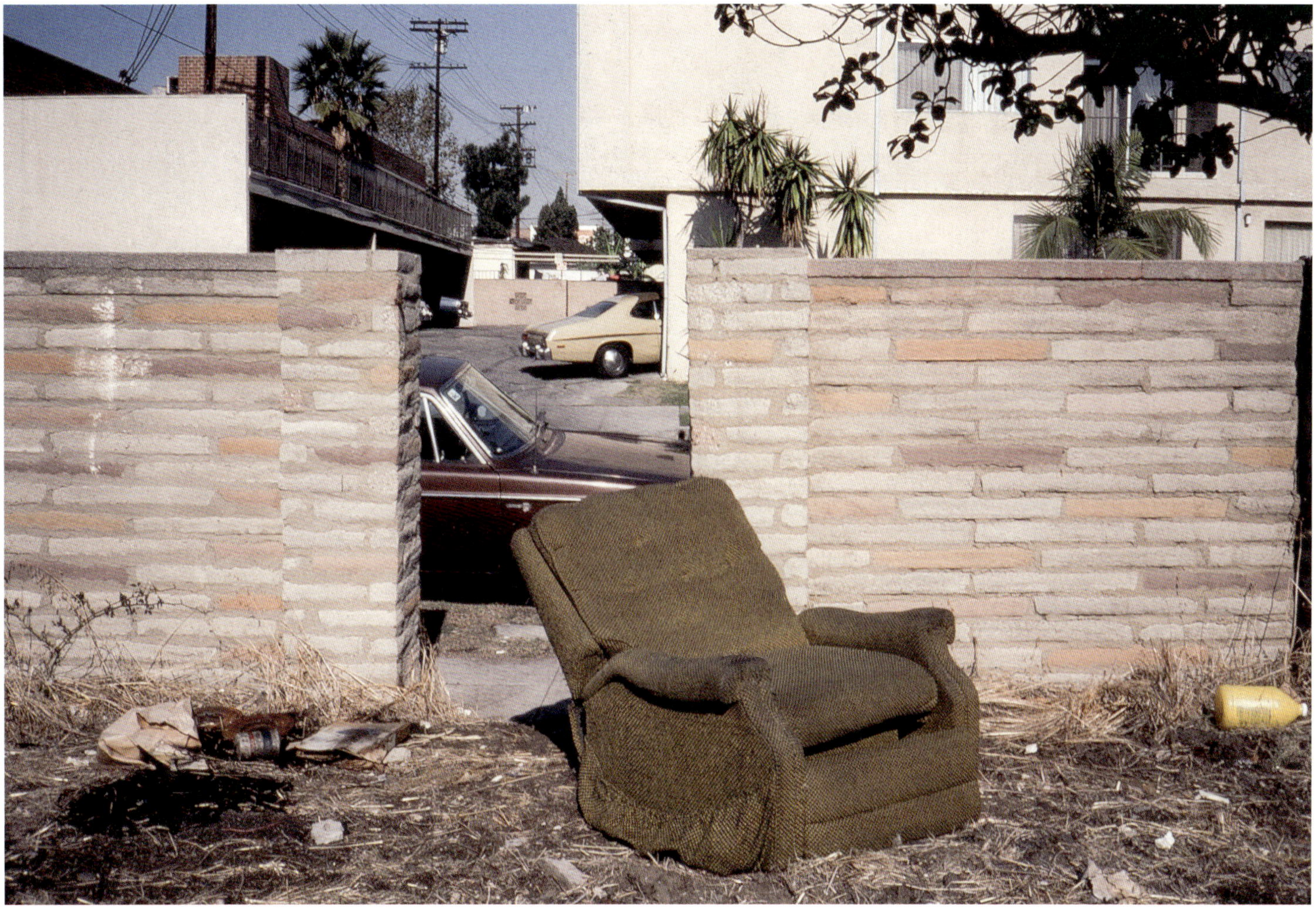

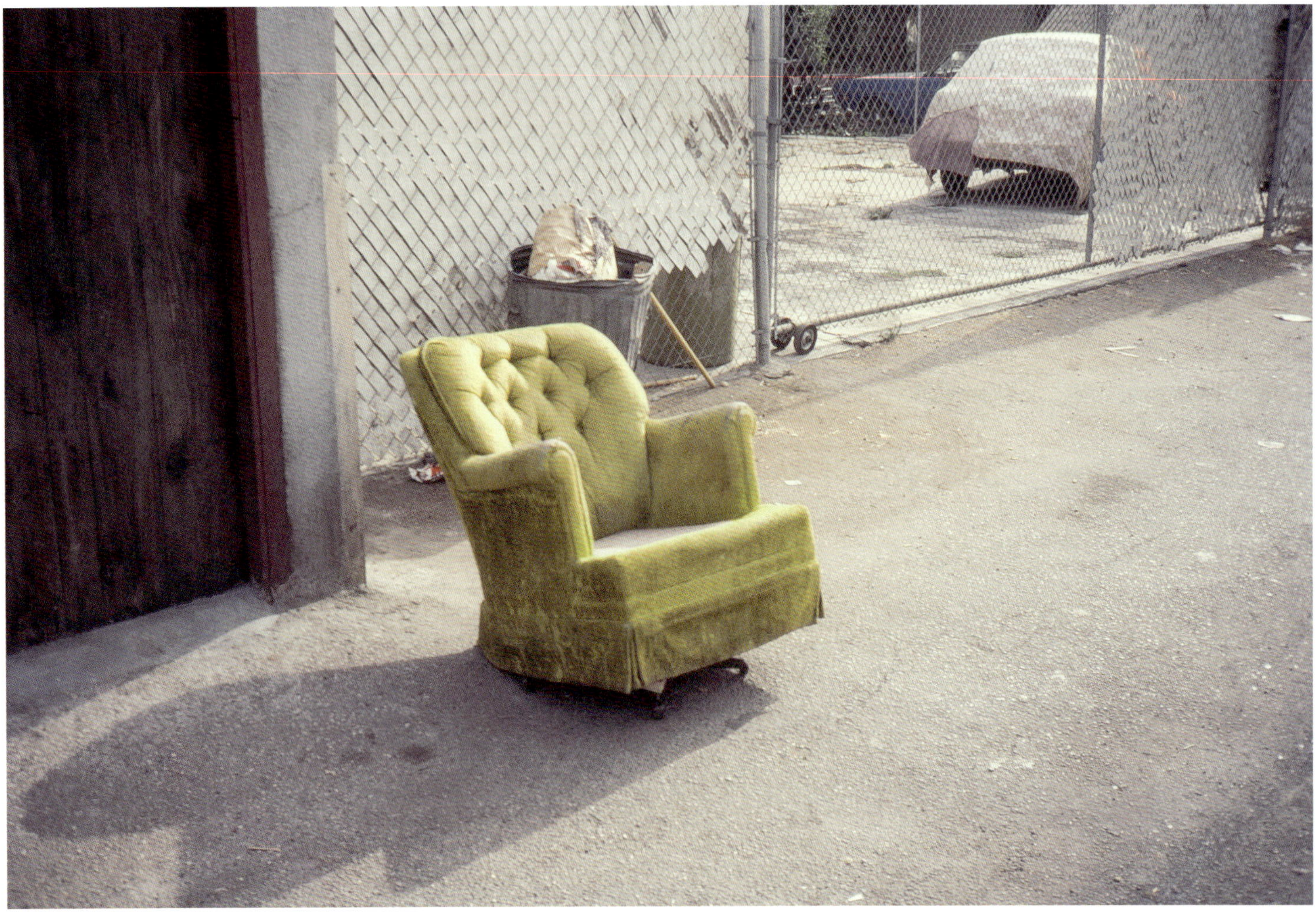

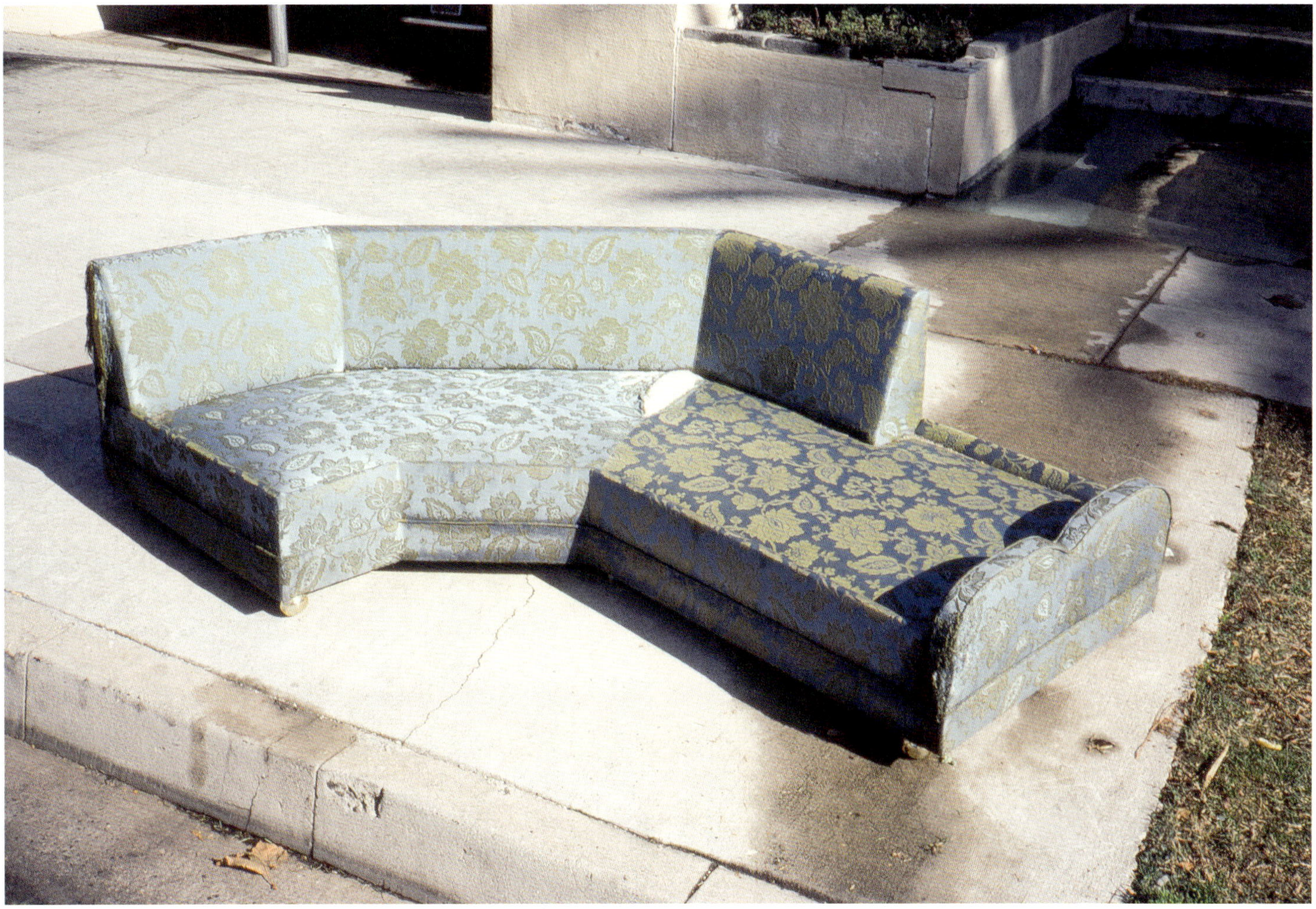

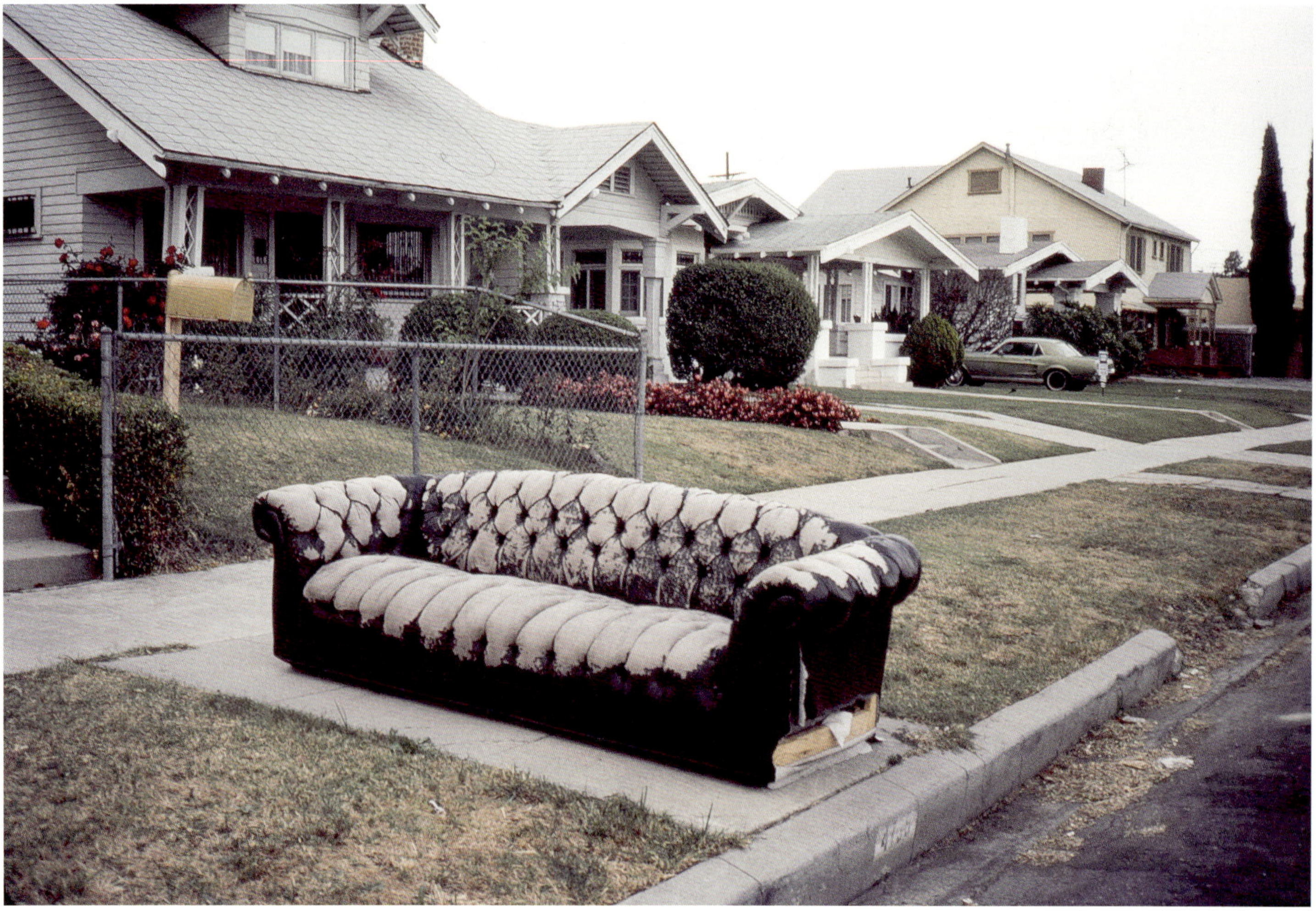

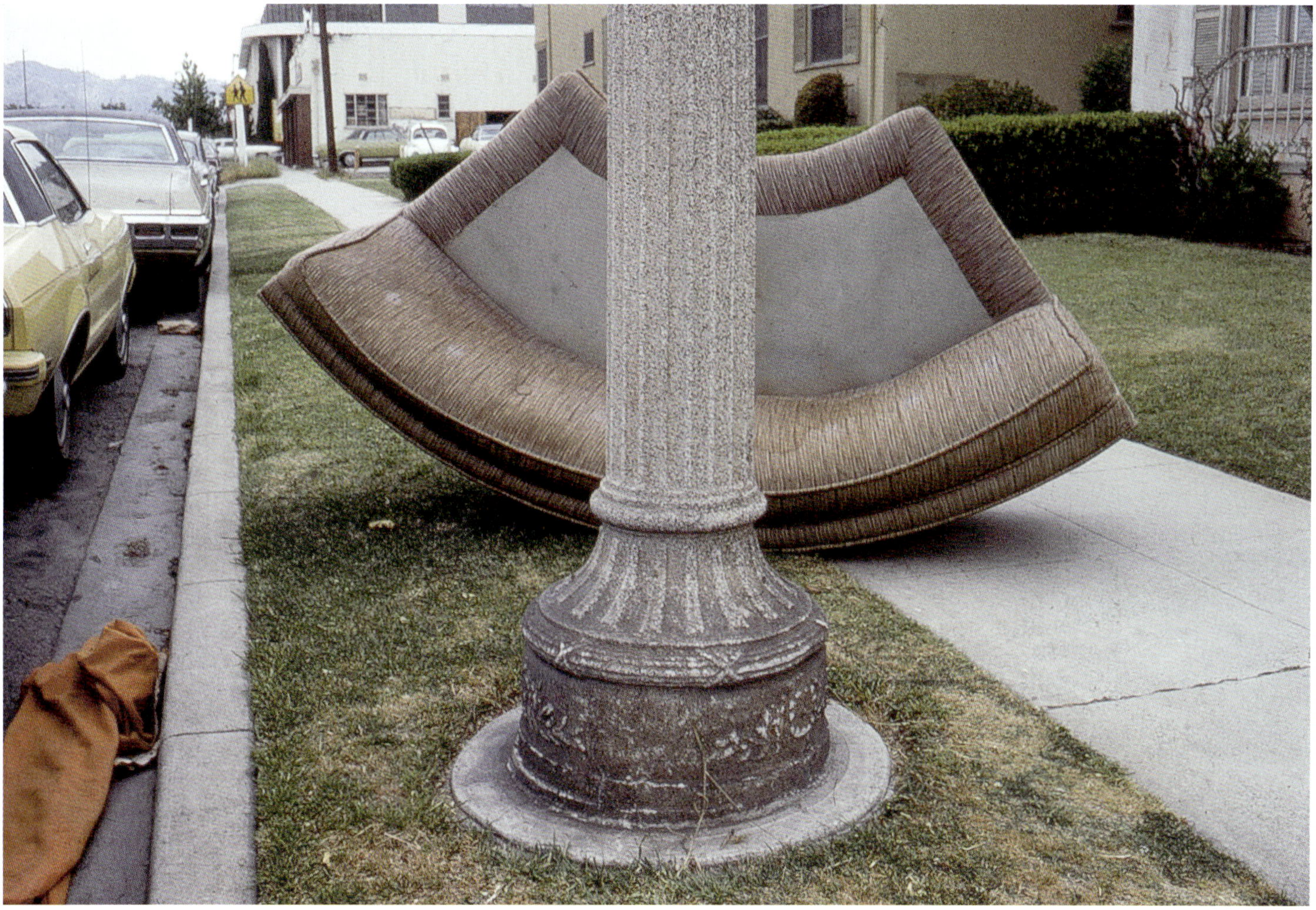

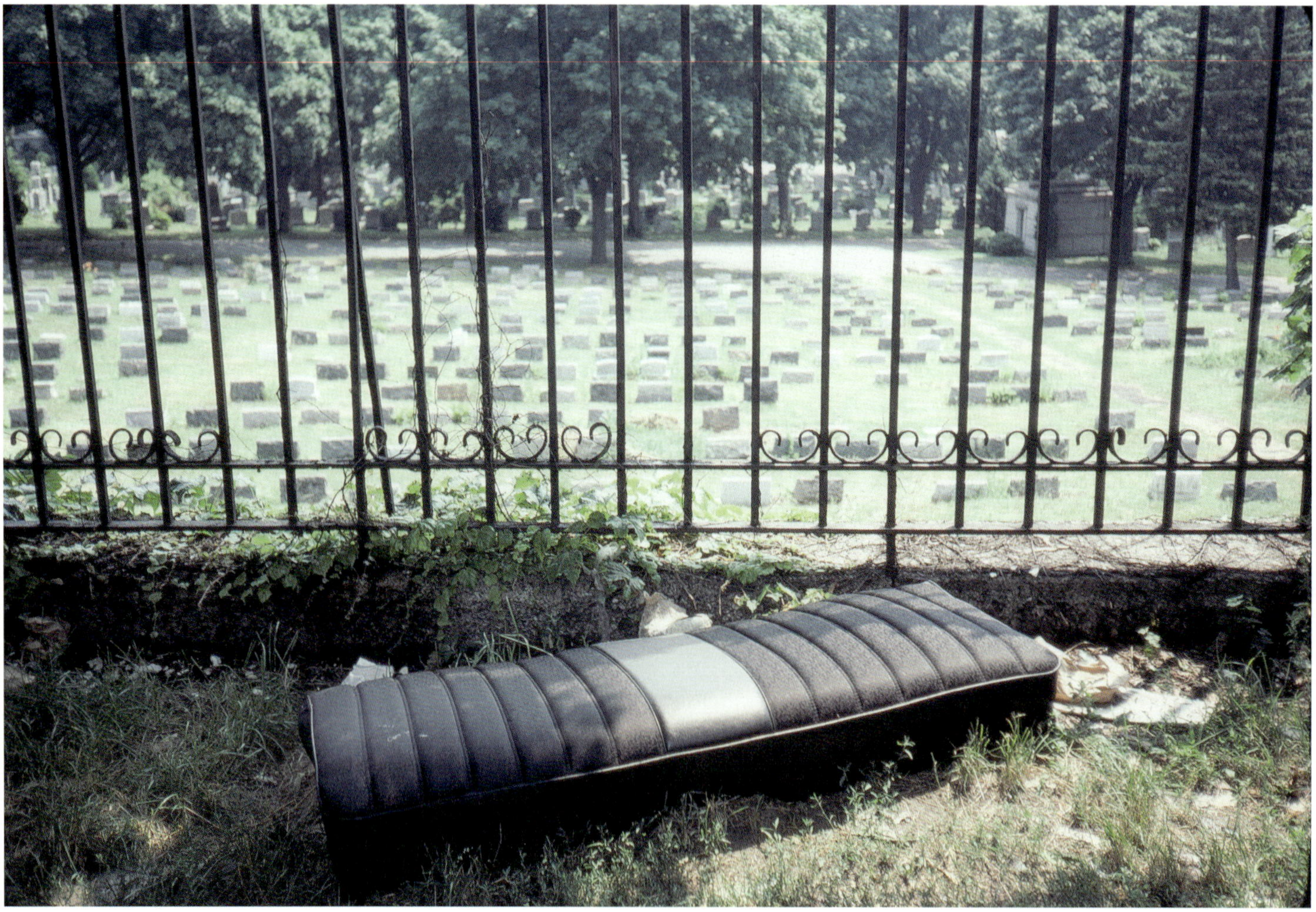

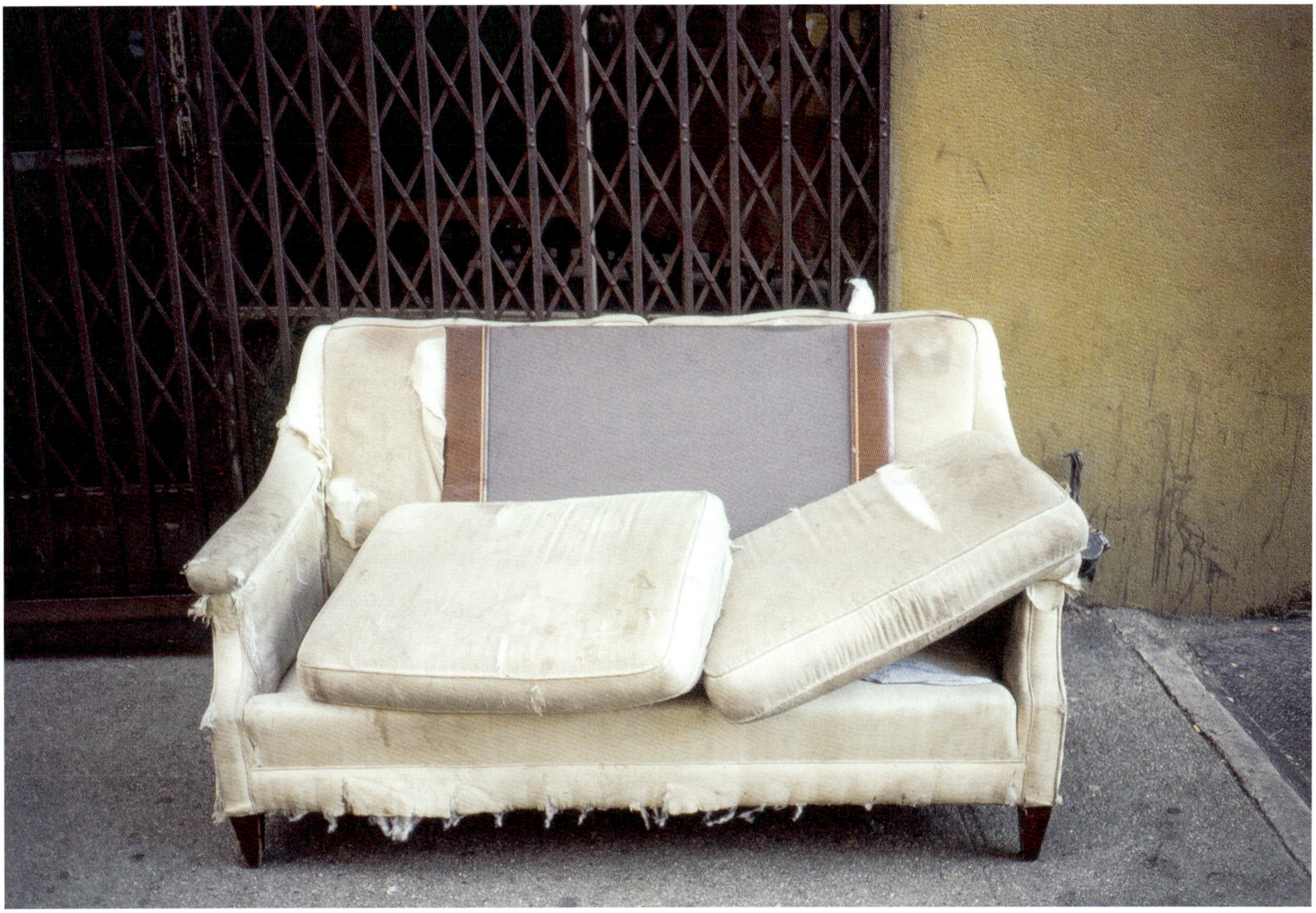

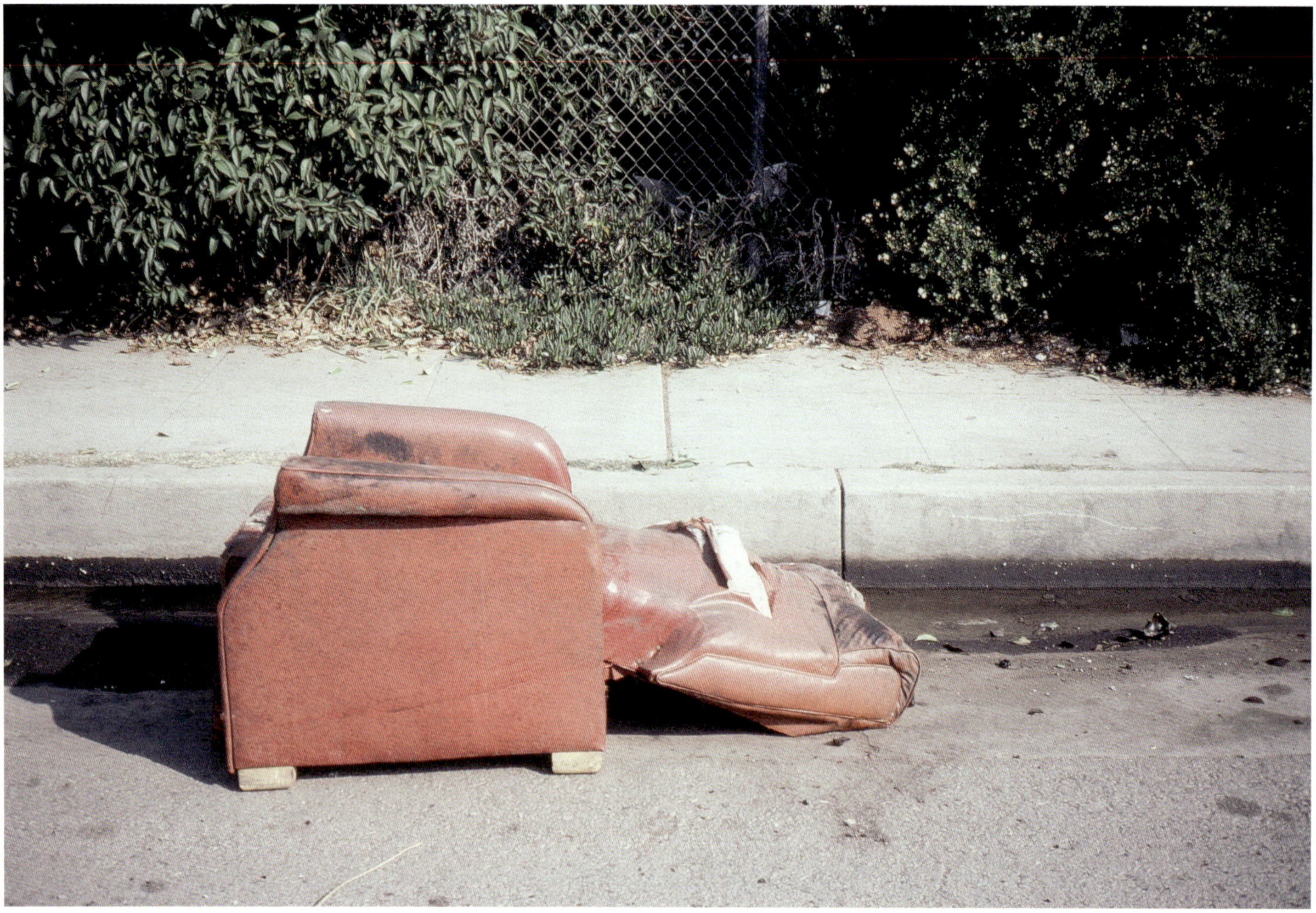

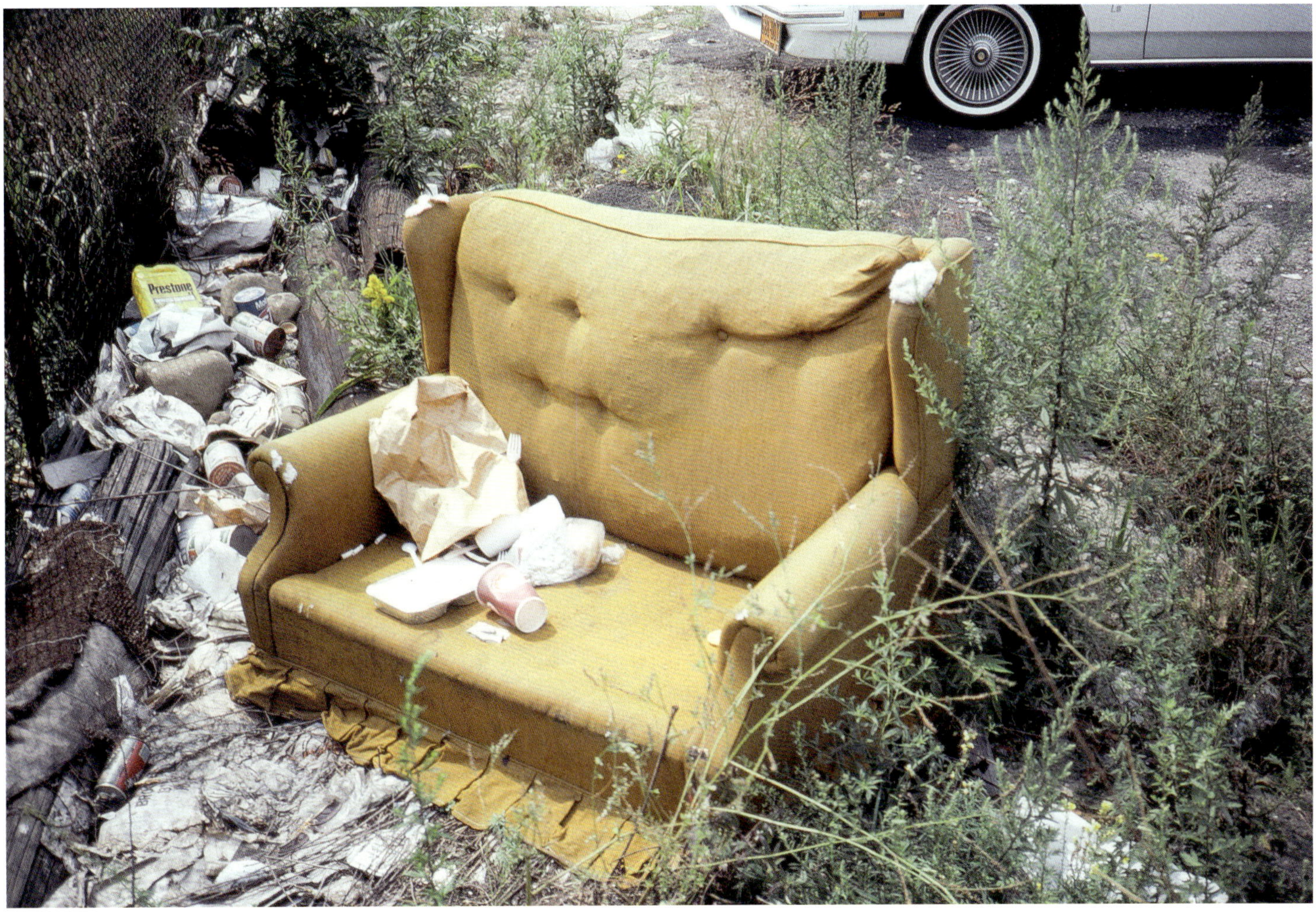
Prestone

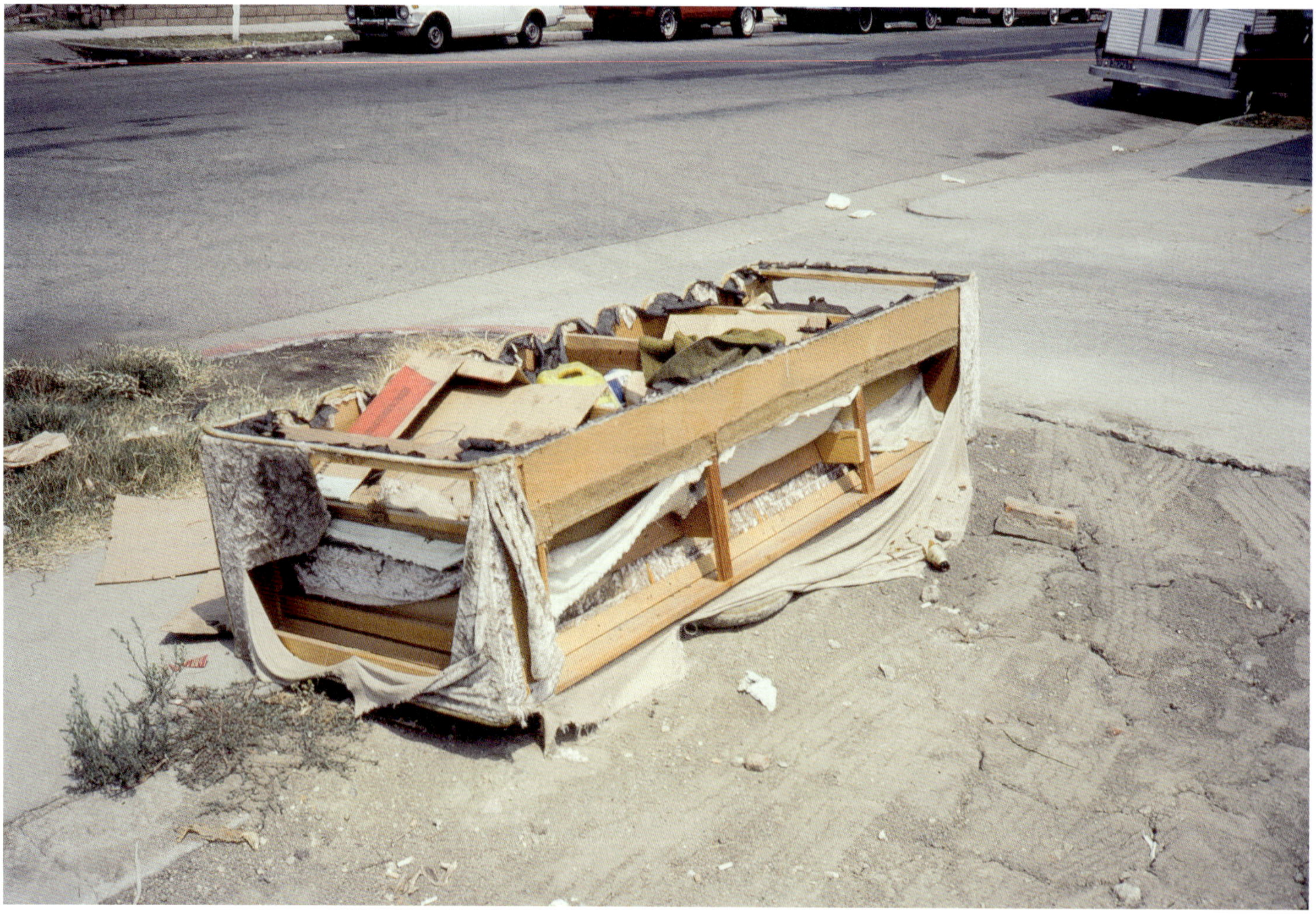

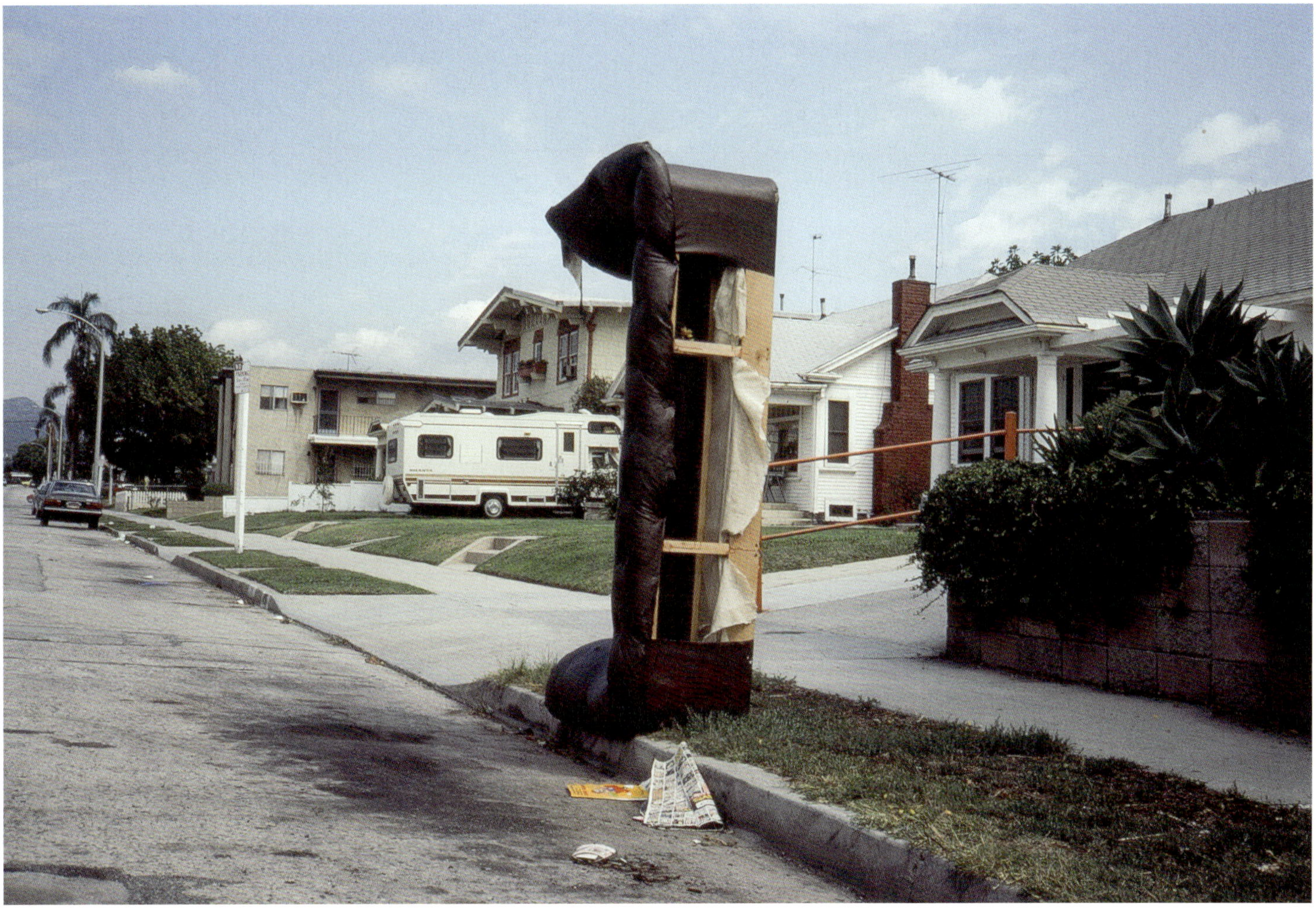

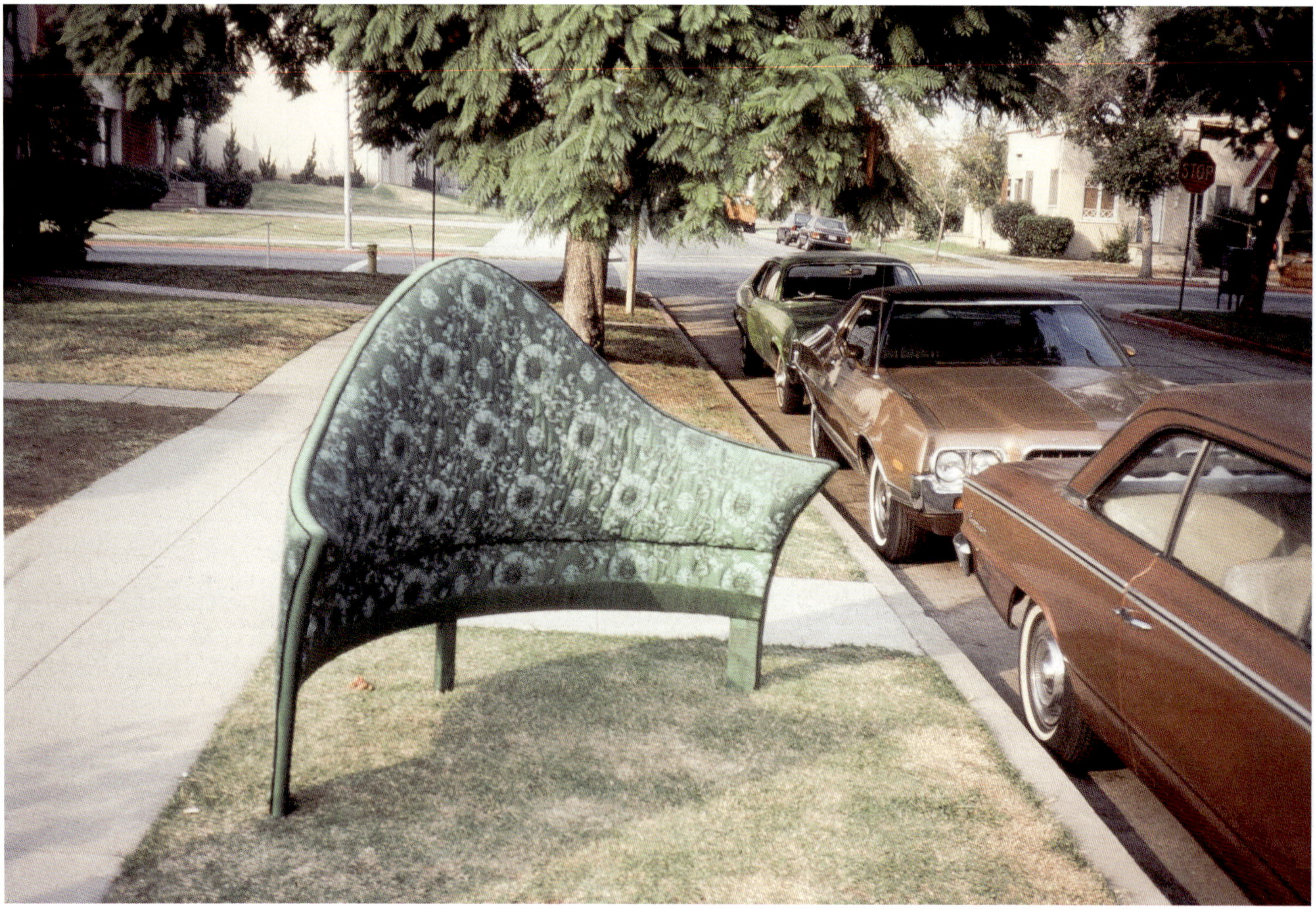
STOP

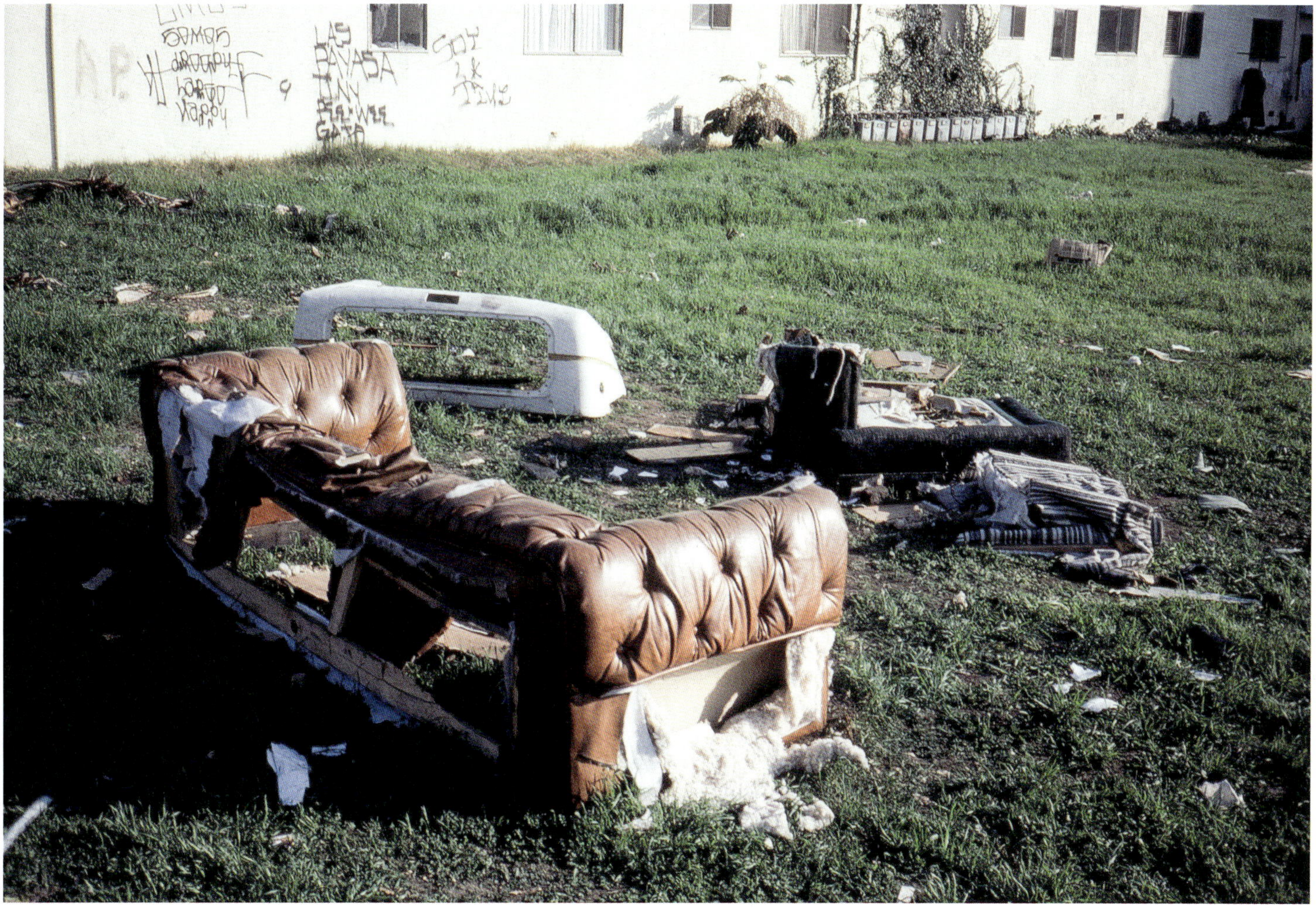

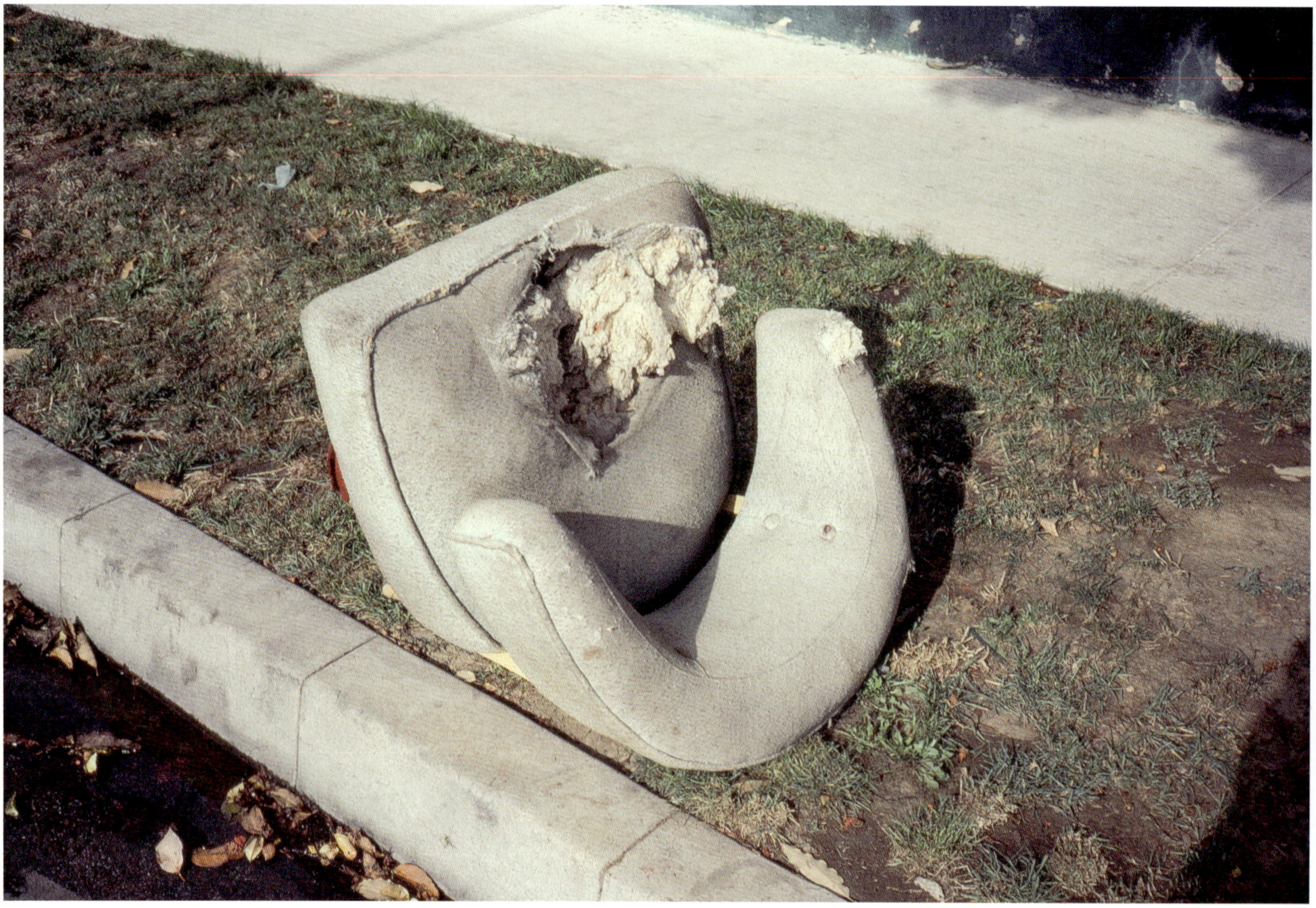

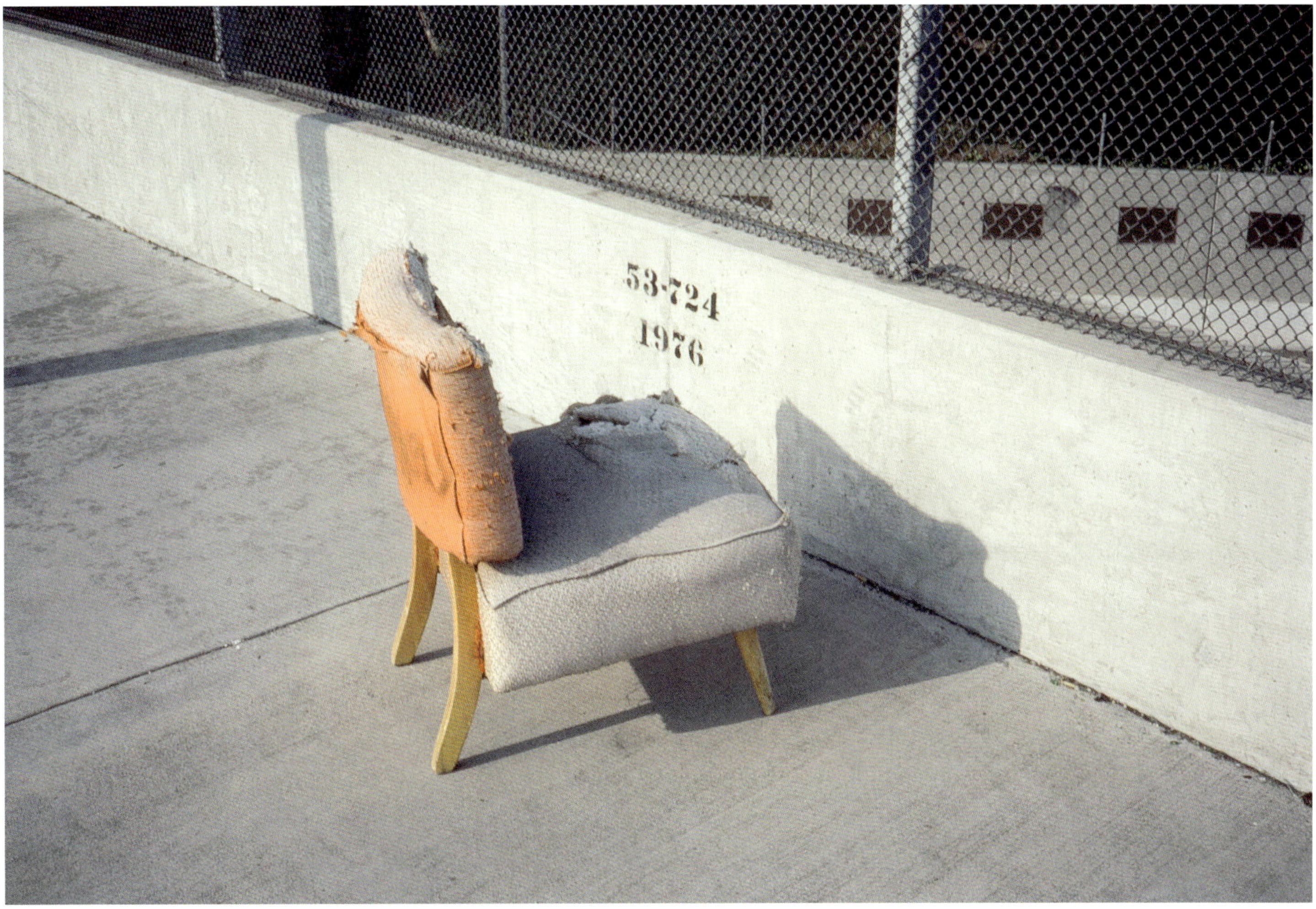
53-724
1976

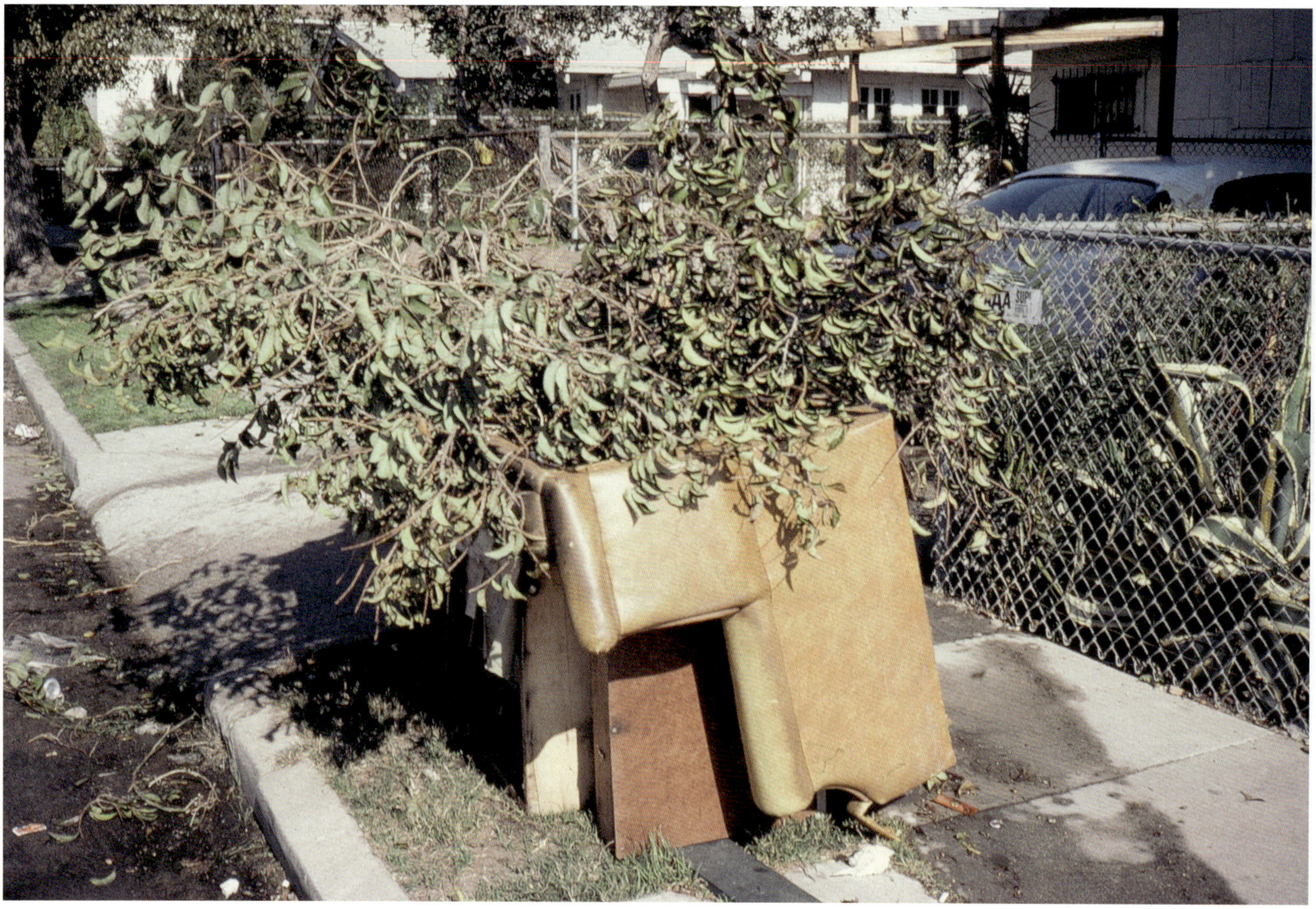

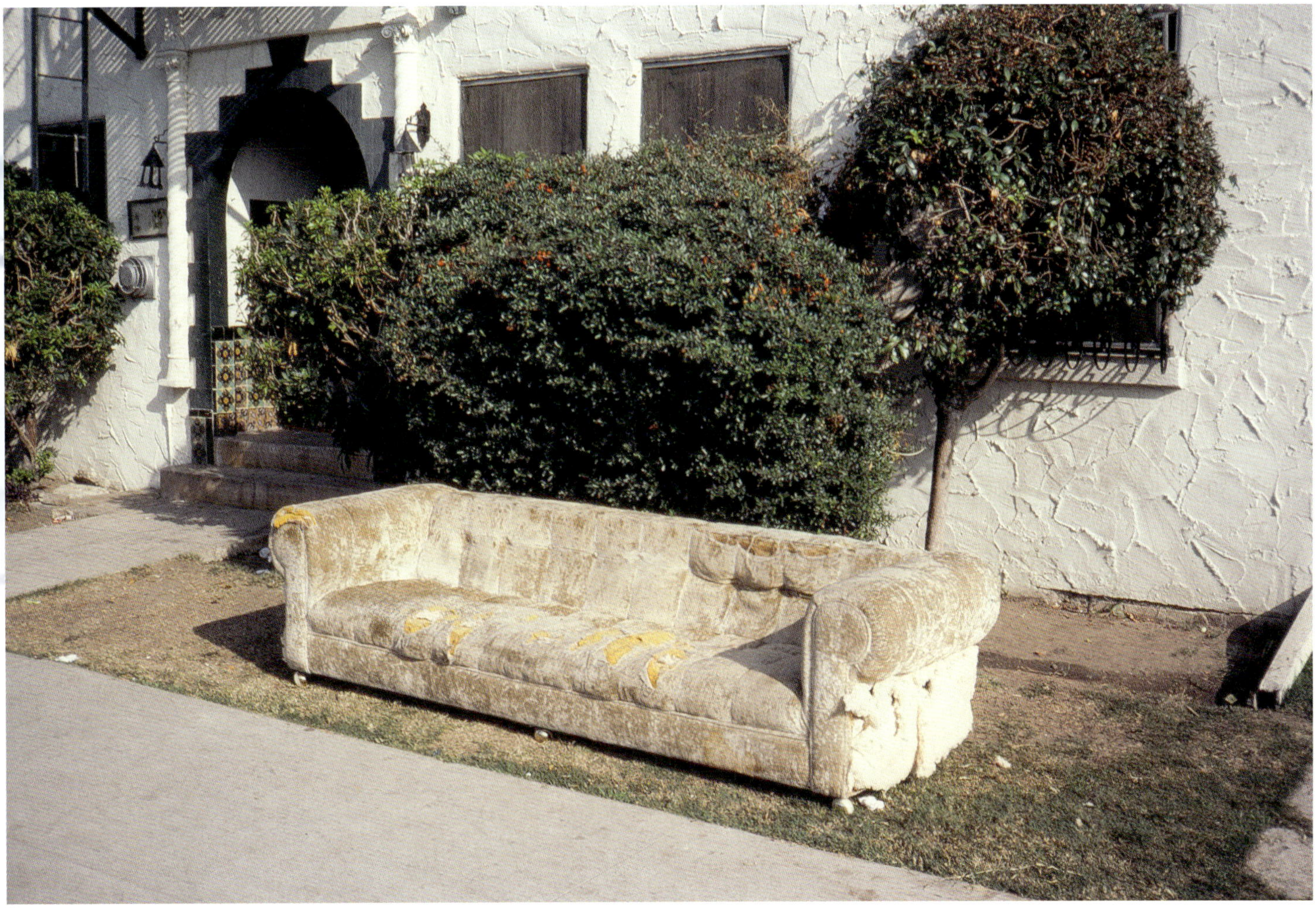

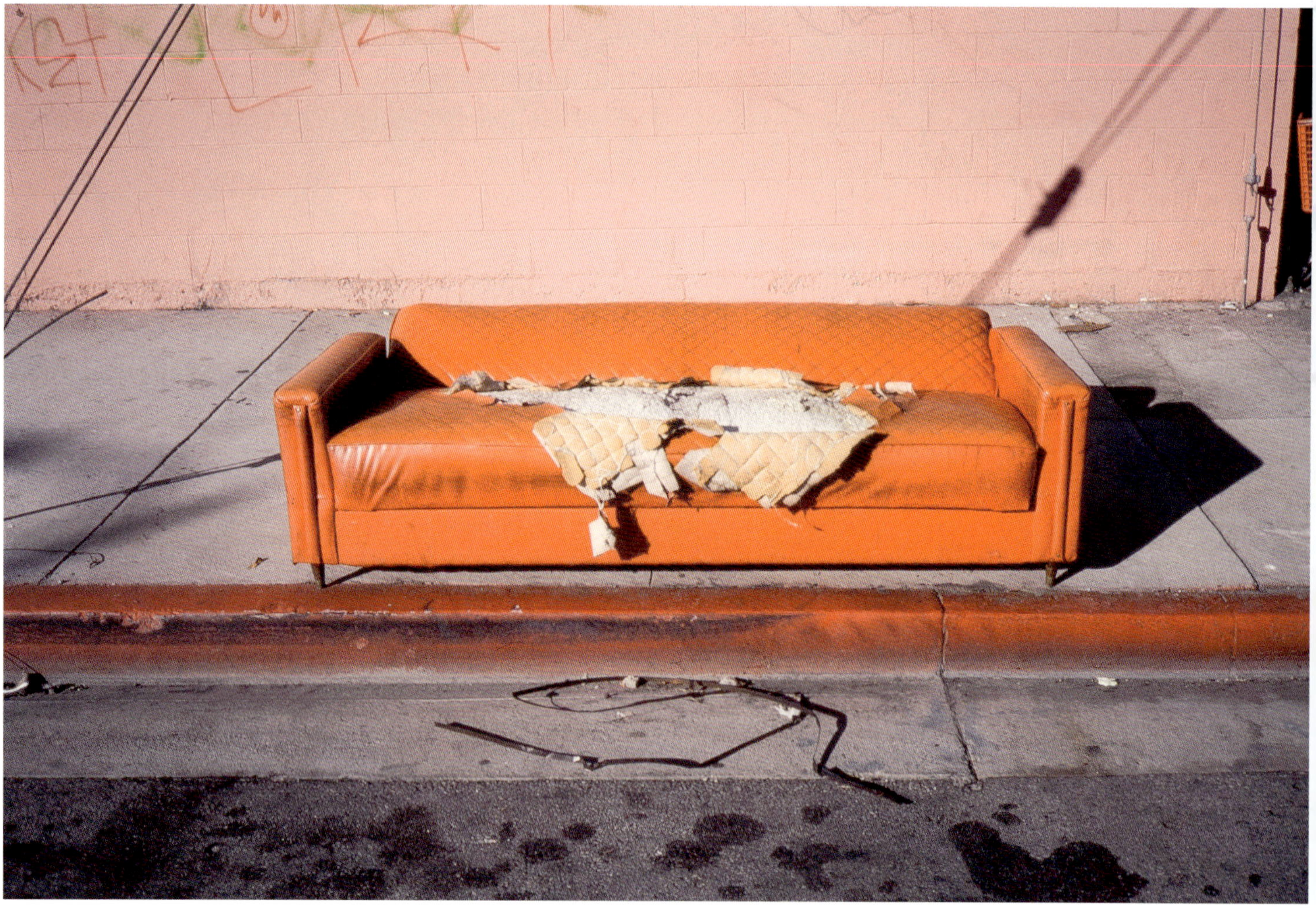

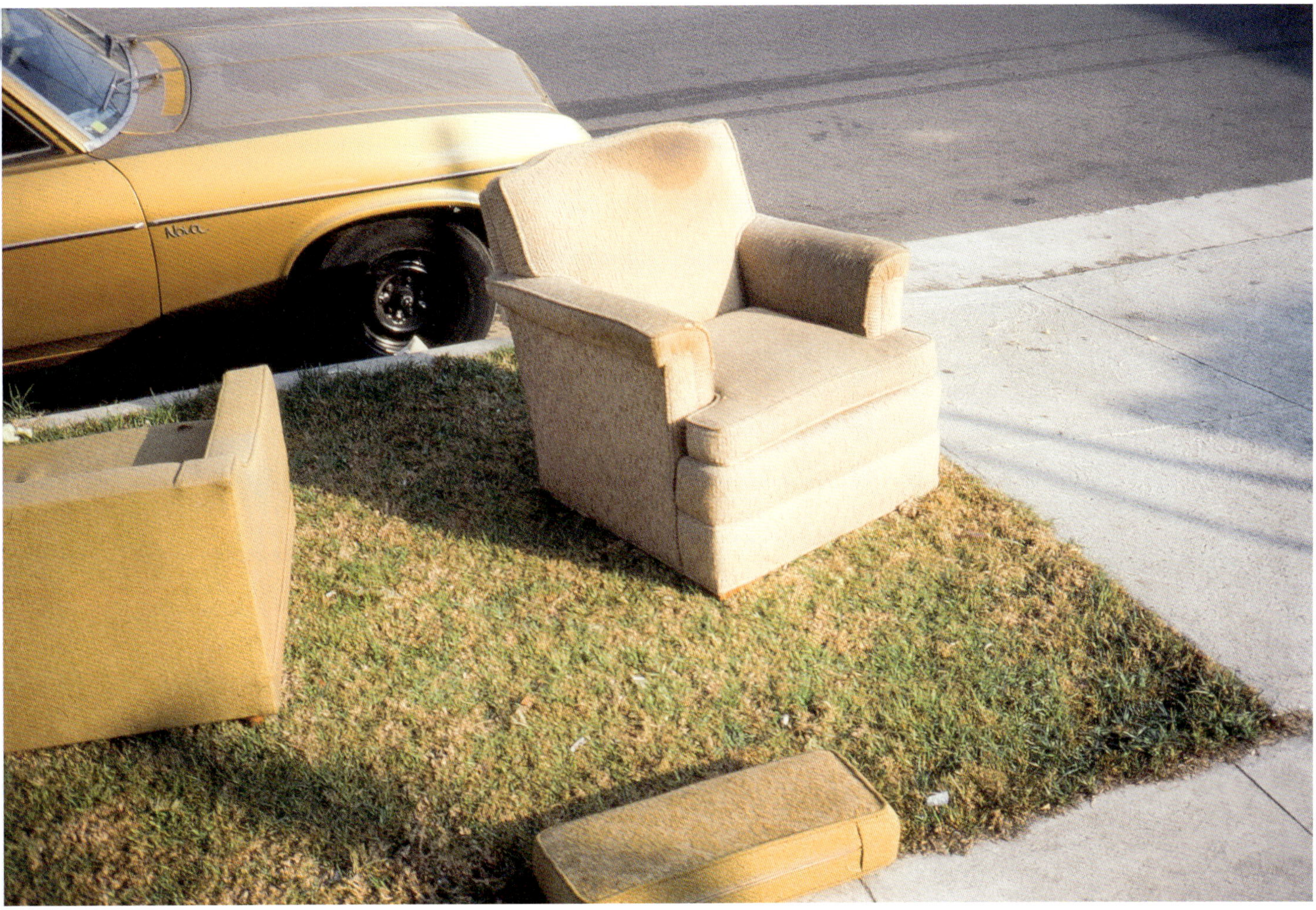

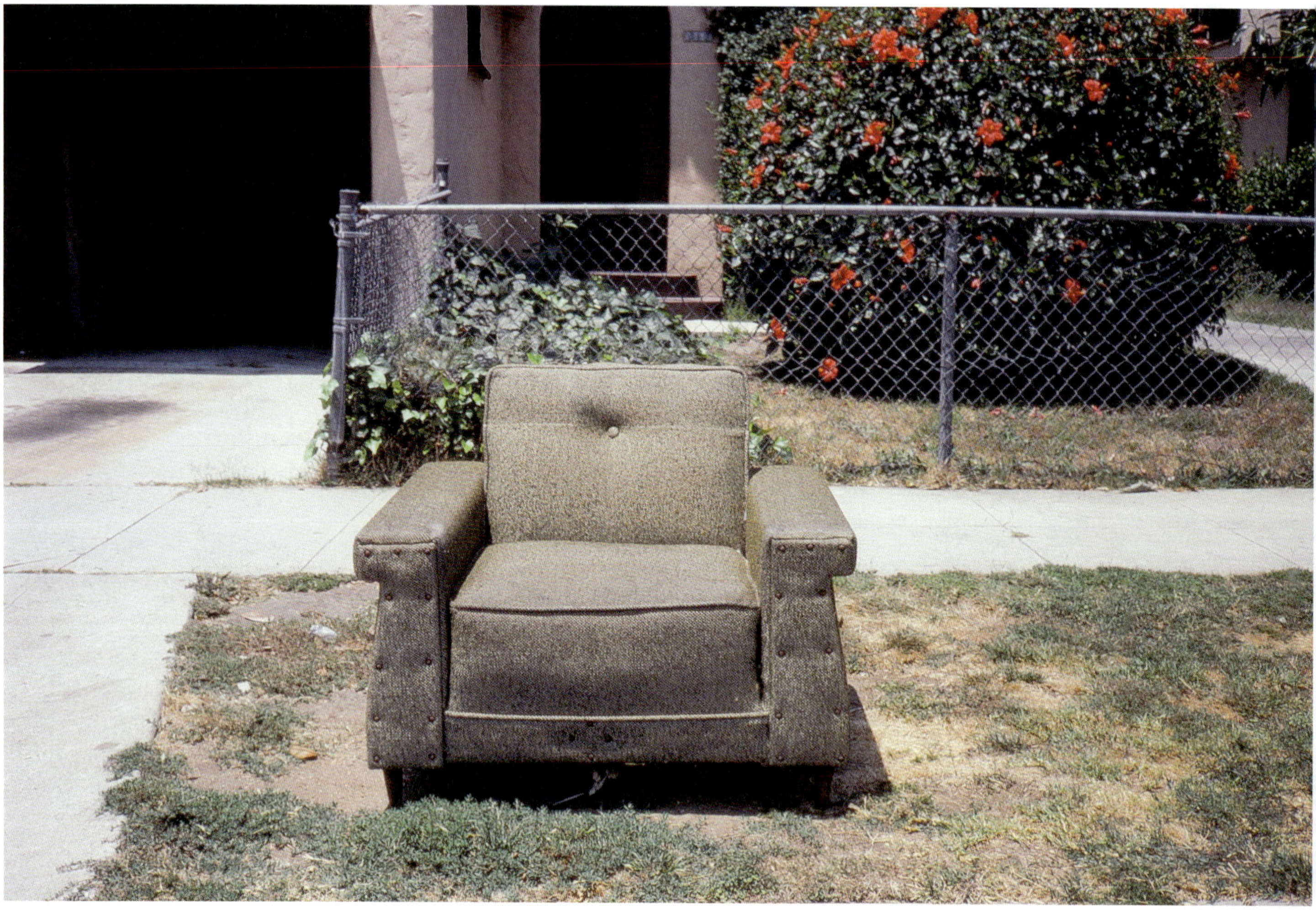

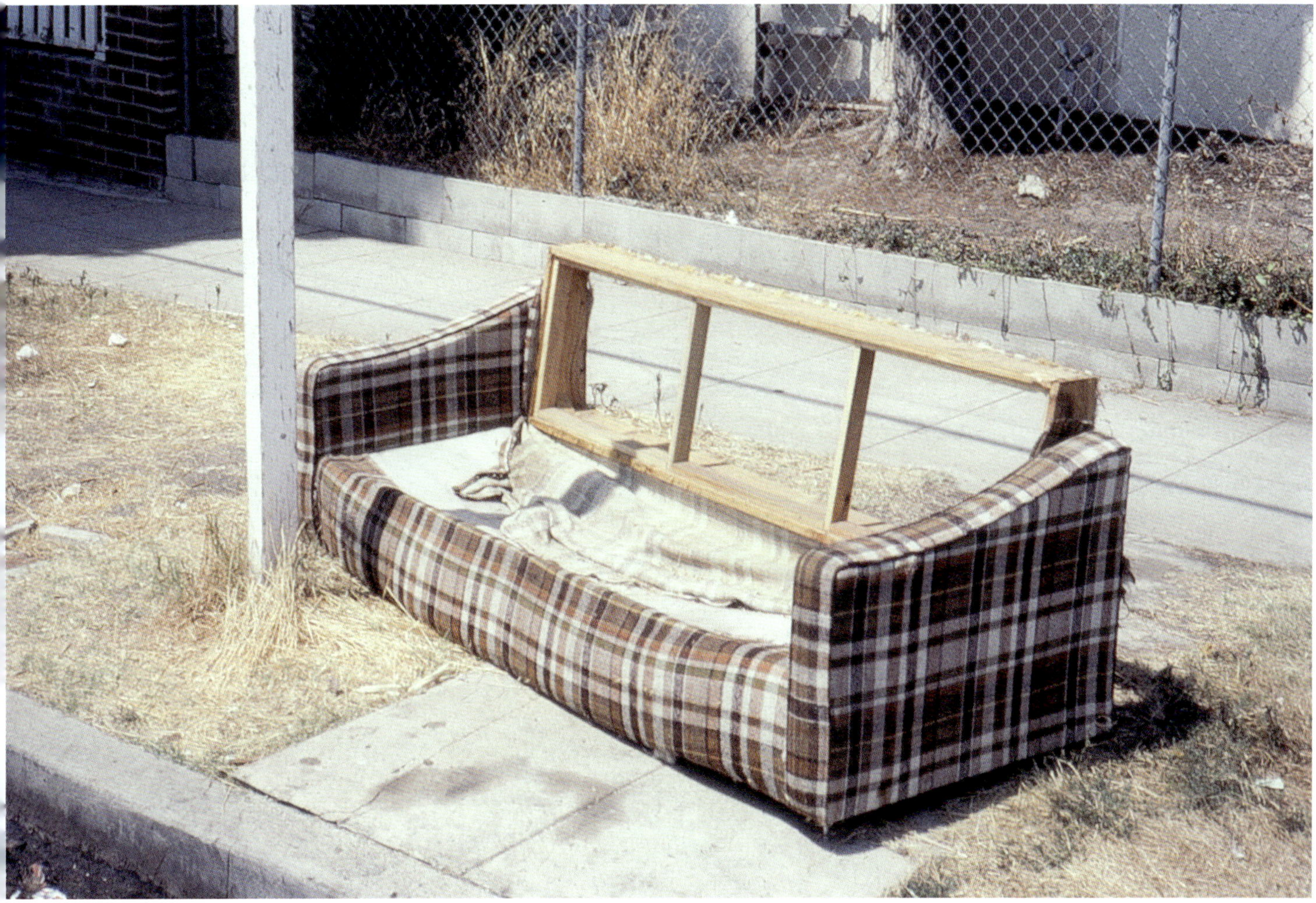

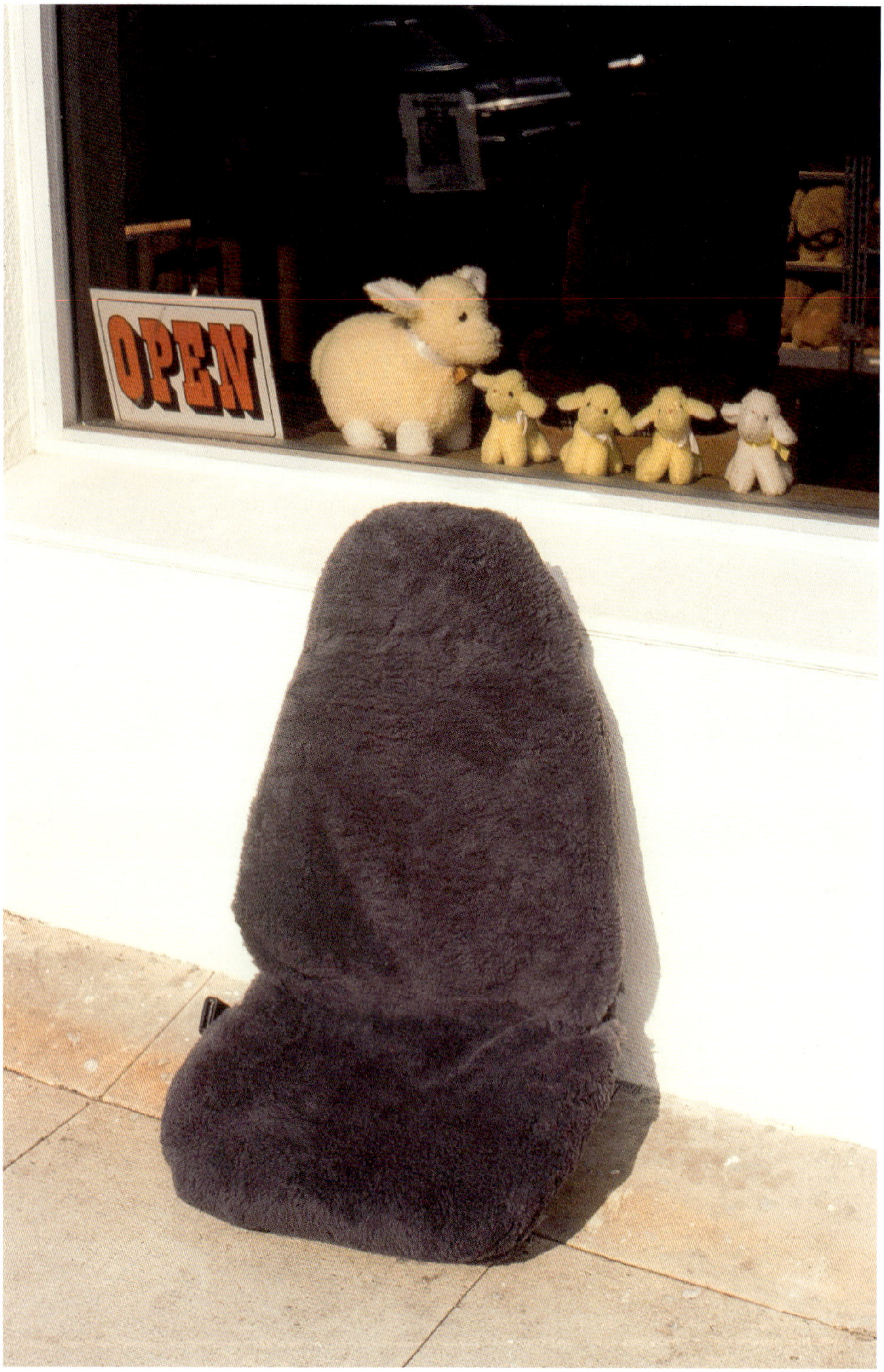
OPEN